Extraordinary Property Investing:

How an ordinary bank teller acquired 151 properties

Felicity Heffernan

OMNE

First Published by OMNE Publishing in 2017

National Library of Australia Cataloguing-in-Publication entry

Creator: Heffernan, Felicity, author.

Title: Extraordinary Property Investing: How an ordinary bank teller acquired 151 properties in less than 10 years/ Felicity Heffernan.

ISBN: 9780994584106 (pbk.)
       9780994584113 (POD)
       9780994584137 (Kindle)
       9780994584144 (ePub)
       9780994584151 (ibooks)

Subjects: Real estate investment – Case studies
Real property – Capital investments – Case studies
Investment analysis
Investments – Case studies

Dewey Number: 332.6324

Editing: Alison Green
Cover design: Julia Kuris
Internal layout ebook and printing: OMNE Publishing

The book is available in print and as an ebook.

TESTIMONIALS

I have known Felicity for over 15 years and during that time she has always delivered to me and my vendor financed clients her very best. I have financed over 76 properties in the past 10 years and to date I have found no one better than Felicity to assist me getting the finance and then managing the entire process from start to finish. Felicity's personal experience as a very successful investor herself has helped me increase my profits and, more importantly, saved heaps of time. Almost all mortgage brokers will tell you they can get the deal for you. Felicity actually can whereas most others fail to deliver because they don't have the experience or skills.

Jeff Muir Property Investor and Business Coach - That's Easy Learning 1300 555 635

Dear Felicity,
Thank you so much for your time and for organising my catch up on the phone yesterday. You cleared my head & I feel a lot closer than I was if I set my mind to it. I should get a good tax return this year & will put it straight on my credit card. Savings set up for $300 a month, not much but as you say it's the pattern / regularity! On to our builders re our potential deal in southwest Sydney. Have a great week, thanks again & I can't wait to call you when I have done those 3 things!!

Jacqui

Dear Felicity,
Just a quick email to thank you. Not only have you saved us thousands of dollars in bank interest, etc, but you are also shouting us to a few good movies!

Len & Sue Farrugia

Dear Felicity,

As a business owner, who values the customer first, it is easy to identify another business that has the same values. It was an absolute pleasure to deal with you all. I know that our refinances would have been super challenging. I also have a sneaky suspicion that there were many hiccups along the way, but you never stressed us with the details. You took on all the stress, sorted the issues without bothering us, and then called with all the great news humbly. You'll probably never told us how many extra miles you went to get it across the line. But please know deep down that we are forever grateful for everything you did for us to get the impossible achieved. You were so honest from the very beginning, so we knew exactly where we stood, with no unbroken promises. We really thought it was going to be the most stressful process, but instead it was actually fun! Thanks for all your genuine support, for the wonderful little cute surprises (movie passes, cheese making kit, cards, and the best follow-up process ever post settlement), and for looking after us like family would. We are actually looking forward to more purchases, which is extremely achievable now as our servicing has increased with the refinances, and the equity releases have allowed us to create even more equity through renovations. We are so honoured to be a client of yours. Thank you from the bottom of our hearts.

Belinda & Marc

I have known Felicity since 2001 when I bought my first home on vendor finance. As a business owner it is really difficult to get finance but Felicity has been my trusted advisor helping me with home loan finance and advice on many aspects of my money. Felicity has assisted me with everything from budgeting to paying off my mortgage quickly and referring us to the right people at the right time for specialist advice. I look forward to many years of continuing to work with Felicity as the results have been amazing.

Chris Everingham Hunter Maintenance and Management

It has been my pleasure to know Felicity since 2011. We met via our mutual interest in alternative home loan financing, an interest we still share today. I've regularly used the services of Felicity's mortgage broking business for my own investment strategies. This has been such a positive experience, I've happily recommended Felicity's services to many of my clients. Without exception, all have been so impressed with her knowledge and professionalism, they too recommend Felicity whenever they get the chance.

Felicity has a passion to improve the financial literacy of the general public and, as I share this passion, we've often worked together over the years, providing finance and investment seminars and workshops.

Felicity believes in a strong, diverse residential lending industry and to this end is the Chairwoman of the Finance Brokers Association of Australia's (FBAA), Vendor Finance Steering Committee. I too am a member of this Committee and can assure you that the Committee is driven from the top ☺

Felicity operates to the highest ethical standard and lives by her business credo, i.e. 'Client First – Always'.

I love this book and know it will assist so many people's financial lives. Enjoy!

Paul Dobson
FBAA Vendor Finance Steering Committee member
Vendor Finance Association of Australia - ex Vice President
Vendor Finance Institute - Director
Australia Credit Licence holder
QLD, NSW, VIC & WA Real Estate Agent licensee

Felicity was instrumental in making our loan happen for us. She was able to get the funds we needed when other institutions that we had been with for 15 years could not. Felicity & her team were fantastic & nothing was too much trouble for them. They kept us informed all through the process. I would recommend her without hesitation.

A & H Trimboli

I've found a true friend
Not one who gave me money
Not one who asked me for favours
Not one who expected anything from me
I found a friend who imparted knowledge freely in the simplest way
In that simple lesson, she has changed my financial world of chaos
You guessed it, that friend is now my MORTGAGE BROKER
With great thanks and appreciation, I would highly recommend Felicity Heffernan for her professional no-nonsense approach.
CLIENT FIRST ALWAYS

Mick Stewart Future founder of the $5.00 per day empire

I am extremely fortunate to have found Felicity after an extensive search for great property investment education. Felicity balances professionalism and fun to provide structured and comprehensive advice in an engaging manner. She has an extensive knowledge, based on experience, which she has channelled into providing people with financial literacy for mortgages. This has enabled me to keep my goals on track and grow my portfolio at an accelerated rate.

Property investment can be a challenging process with many associated risks. Felicity's attention to detail and strong ethical nature ensures that all information is accurate, unbiased and truthful.

I highly recommend Felicity as your trusted property investment loan advisor.

Karen Ruppert Property Investor

Felicity is a most extraordinary business person and investor. As her accountant, I have watched her grow from her earlier days as a budding property investor into the business success she is today. Her courage, tenacity, tact, expertise and professionalism is truly inspiring.

Bruce Whiting Business Artisans Pty Ltd

Felicity Heffernan walks her talk. She is a very experienced vendor financer and mortgage broker who loves to help people move forward and secure the great Aussie dream of home ownership. After 151 vendor finance deals, Felicity knows her stuff and I have dealt with her personally with buyers trying to purchase homes. This book is a must-read for anyone wanting to be a property investor. .

Janine Reynolds Beyond Sales Pty Limited

Just imagine if you could have a one to one with a first-rate property investment guru.

A guru who is willing to share her knowledge with you on how to buy your first investment property and how to build a property portfolio on solid foundations.

That investment guru is Felicity, and in this book she tells you more about the nitty gritty about property investment than almost anyone I know.

Personally, I would like to think that I am a Level 5 – Sophisticated Investor, who loves using vendor finance strategies both to buy and to sell property.

I'm hoping that you can all join myself and Felicity on Level 5, and receive passive property income in excess of what we earn in our day jobs.

Anthony (Tony) Cordato Property Investment Lawyer

ACKNOWLEDGEMENTS

I have been incredibly fortunate to have met many teachers and others in my life that have supported and encouraged me to be my best self. I offer a most sincere thank you to all…

Firstly, to my parents who instilled in me solid financial habits and gave me a strong foundation for my journey in life; to my husband, Greg, who has been by my side since I was 16 and has always been my love, my rock and the voice of reason when life becomes challenging; to our two beautiful girls, Laura and Courtney, who inspire me every day and are now young adults forging their own path to make a difference in the world, something I am extremely proud of; to my brothers and sisters and extended family, for your constant love and support.

To my staff at Property Loan Advisor, Ruth and Alyce, I could not ask for a better team to support me. Both of you are amazing and I am eternally grateful for the work that you do.

To the people that have supported me in my business life. To Bruce Whiting my accountant, my guiding light in the accounting and tax world; to Tony Cordato my lawyer and wonderful trusted advisor on all things legal; to Paul Dobson whom I have had the unique pleasure to work alongside to bring professionalism and credibility to the vendor finance industry; to Peter White and the team at the Finance Brokers Association of Australia for the amazing support you have given me personally to support the vendor finance industry; and to the wonderful people who assist me in my mortgage broking business. The list is long, but notably Suzanne Hemsworth from La Trobe Financial, Noushig Megerditchian from LoanKit, Jonathan Valentino from RESIMAC and Heather Gallagher from BOQ, you guys make it so much easier for me to serve our clients.

To the people who helped me with this book: the team from Key Person of Influence, notably Glen Carlson and Andrew Griffiths. To Alison J Green for editing; Julia Kuris for book cover design; Sharon

Westin-Shaw for graphic design; and Andrew Akratos for layout and printing. To my daughter Courtney Heffernan for the illustrations. To the team at Woo Hoo for the wonderful work you do with my hair and make-up, especially Makayla Frazer, Annie Hake and Emma Hutchinson. To Glenn Kelly for your amazing photography and your enduring determination to work as a photographer even though you are legally blind. You are a huge inspiration to me because you show that we can do anything.

To the countless number of wonderful people that I have not mentioned by name, thank you for being in my life.

And finally, a very special mention to John Burley, my teacher, mentor and friend. I am so incredibly grateful for your vision, inspiration, commitment and passion to educate the world on how to be financially free. It is your values I want to emulate and pass on through this book. The knowledge you shared has impacted my life immensely for the better, and I owe you a debt of gratitude that is beyond measure.

Extraordinary Property Investing.

TABLE OF CONTENTS

FOREWORD

It is my tremendous honor to write the foreword for my dear friend Felicity Heffernan's book *Extraordinary Property Investing*. The book tells the story, along with amazing tips and how-to's, of how Felicity went from being a Mum and part-time teller to becoming one of the great property investors in Australia!

Felicity is an inspiration to women and men all across Australia. She has spent countless hours teaching, mentoring and speaking, sharing her wisdom and educating so many people on how to become successful property investors.

When I first met Felicity, she was as new as it gets. Her journey and her passion for growth and learning are truly remarkable. You will learn how she set aside 'negative gearing' and amassed a fortune while building a portfolio of 'positive cash flow' properties.

Felicity is an 'extraordinary' person and I know you will benefit greatly from her knowledge and wisdom in *Extraordinary Property Investing*.

I am proud to count Felicity as one of my friends and as a peer in property investing. As you say down under she is truly a 'legend'!

John Burley Professional investor and author of the #1 best sellers. *Money Secrets of the Rich and Powerful Changes*

INTRODUCTION

Many people seek out property investment as a vehicle to financial freedom. Property is something that most people believe they understand, as opposed to shares or commodities. That said, most people are 'sold' investment properties and not really educated on all facets of property investing. Worse still, they are taught that saving tax should be their primary objective. In reality, this can lead to huge negative monthly cash flows which, in turn, lead to disillusionment and possibly even financial ruin. Other important areas often overlooked by aspiring property investors include establishing the foundations for successful property acquisition and developing the mindset required to grow a property portfolio. After all, it is essentially a business and as such, requires all the skills and business acumen that would be required to run a successful business enterprise.

Having acquired 151 properties in a 10-year period, I have discovered what is possible and I know what works and what doesn't. I didn't intentionally set out to acquire so many properties, in fact the original goal was just 10. At the time this goal was regarded as very audacious. I found that the acquisition and possession of investment property was the easy bit. What really required work and stretched me were foundation and accumulation, both essential for success. These were the areas that required a mindset of development and growth.

I have used my personal experience, education and lightbulb moments to develop a comprehensive four-step framework to get you started and to keep you going as a property investor. The framework is holistic and addresses the often forgotten and not-so-sexy aspects of property investing that are so often overlooked, yet absolutely vital to success. It is one thing to go out and buy investment properties, however if your personal financial foundation is not strong, this is the quickest way to financial ruin. Another major element that is often overlooked is mindset. To demonstrate this point, think about all the people who have won substantial amounts on Lotto or Powerball. How many of them are financially independent five years after their winnings? The answer is that most of them have lost their fortune because they didn't develop the mindset to manage the fortune or learn to be a good steward of the money.

So what prevents people from being financially free? Why can't they get started and if they do, why don't they keep going? Why do some end up in financial ruin if they attempt to invest in property? The following concerns are what most people face when it comes to property investing:

- They haven't learnt to manage their own personal finances to work for them.
- They fear debt as a bad thing and not as a tool of leverage.
- They don't know where to start.
- They are afraid that something will go wrong.
- They listen to the wrong people, who often have zero experience in property investing.
- They feel they don't have enough knowledge.
- They don't believe enough in themselves to become financially free.

So how does one overcome any one or a combination of these daunting concerns? My framework covers the **four key areas in the property investment process** that, when implemented together, will ensure the aspiring property investor has the tools to overcome any of the concerns listed and the confidence to build a property portfolio.

The four areas are these:

1. **Setting a Foundation** – knowing where you stand personally and getting your own personal finances in order. Automating your own personal money system so that you have that area of your life under control. Understanding what level of investor you currently are and what level of investor you aspire to be. Choosing a property niche that suits you. You may be fantastic at structuring deals for cash flow but completely inept with a hammer and paint brush in the renovation

niche or vice versa. Getting the foundation correct will change your life.

2. **Acquisition** – learning how to do market research as a valuable skill for ascertaining good deals in the market. Learning about the tools available to help you make informed decisions. Learning how to analyse the numbers – that vary across different property niches - is vital in finding out what you are prepared to pay for a property. Learning tips and strategies on how to submit offers and negotiate the purchase of a property, some of which can save you thousands in holding costs.

3. **Possession –** learning how to take possession of a property; often you can take possession and have the property making you money prior to actually owning it. Learning cost-effective tips for preparing the property so that it produces maximum returns for your portfolio. Learning what it takes to develop effective property management; this is an area that can leave the aspiring property investor disillusioned if they try to do it themselves or employ a poor property manager. Learning how to find a competent property manager so your time is leveraged and focused on the task of acquiring the property.

4. **Accumulation –** Building a strong team of professionals to support you and understand what you are trying to achieve as you grow. The actual accumulation of property resembles a cookie cutter because the system is the same for one property and for multiple properties; it is your financial position that becomes more and more complex and requires sophisticated members on your team to help manage your growth. Learning to understand lag and how it can impact dramatically on the accumulation phase. Some people buy into the idea that you will become a millionaire overnight when you purchase an investment property; nothing could be further from the truth. It is the properties that are purchased as part of a plan that are going to contribute to your financial success and the longer you have been implementing the plan, the bigger the results that you will

see. Learning to develop the right investor mindset will serve you not only in your property investment life but also in your personal life. Not everything is smooth sailing 100% of the time, but having the right attitude when things are rough allows you to course-correct much more efficiently.

Extraordinary Property Investing: How an ordinary bank teller acquired 151 properties in less than 10 years is a road map for the aspiring property investor to help you build a solid financial foundation and acquire multiple properties.

CHAPTER 1

Where It All Began

I was born in September 1962 (good vintage), the eldest of seven children, and raised in Glenbrook, a sleepy little town in the lower Blue Mountains of New South Wales. My father was a very staunch Catholic man who ruled with a firm hand to keep all of us in check. My mother, who was overworked and under-resourced, was an extremely good budgeter who managed the extraordinarily lean household finances.

My father was employed by the public service for all his working life as a manager at The Public Trustee. I never really knew what he did exactly, just that he looked after dead people's stuff. The advice that he gave all of as we were growing up was that if we studied hard, got good grades and found a government job with a good superannuation plan, we would be set for life. After all, that was what he did and it worked for him. In fact, I remember that when he retired he had one of those great superannuation plans known as defined benefits that was indexed for life. If he passed first, Mum would get five eighths of that payment. His goal when he retired was to outlive what he accumulated and he has achieved that goal! We all must have paid attention to his advice, as we all started with government jobs when we left school.

Growing up, I use to think how boring it was to live in Glenbrook, but now when I look back I think how idyllic the lifestyle was. My first memory of anything really exciting happening in Glenbrook was *The Sound of Music* motion picture being screened and the whole town being so excited. To this day it is still my favourite movie. I remember Mum thought it was a good idea to make play clothes out of the curtains, like Maria did for the Von Trapp children. I just wanted to die of embarrassment at the very thought of it. Imagine all my brothers and sisters wearing the same clothes made from curtain material! Mum was a good seamstress and made just about everything we wore.

Mum was always on the hunt for a money-saving tip and she was the queen of bargains. She would regularly drive to Fielders Bakery in St Mary's and jostle with the pig farmers to get the best of the day-old bread for five cents a loaf. She would often get 50 loaves of bread that would be distributed among three other families. Every Tuesday morning Mum would drive to Franklins in Penrith as it was the cheapest grocery store and Tuesday was bargain day. When Franklins released their no-frills brand Mum was their biggest advocate. If there was a bargain to be found, Mum would find it.

Mum used to rustle us out of the house by 9 am and we were always told to be home before dark. We lived very close to the national park where I spent most of my childhood roaming with the neighbour kids, especially during the school holiday breaks. There were some great swimming holes known as the Jelly Bean Pool and the Blue Pool, bush tracks and caves. There was one cave known as Red Hands Cave with a lot of Aboriginal hand paintings on the wall. As kids we use to hike out there and mix up the clay that was close by, dip the palms of our hands and place our hand prints on the cave wall to imitate the ones that were already there. Imagine being able to do that now! Red Hands Cave is now fenced off and it is regarded as one of the best showcases of Aboriginal rock art in the area.

My parents' first car was a Vanguard, and my earliest memories was Mum, heavily pregnant, having to use a crank handle to start the car as this particular model didn't have a starter motor. Dad thought it would be a good idea to change the colour of the car from black to white – no problems a little bit of white house paint did the job! They later upgraded to a station wagon and as more kids came along they eventually upgraded to a bright yellow nine-seater Combi van as the seatbelt laws were starting to be introduced. This was a huge expense and I remember dad having to negotiate hard with the bank manager to let him go into overdraft to afford the car. Putting it another way, it was not an option for my mother to be without a car as she relied on it heavily for the shopping and transporting us around, so he had little choice but to be really convincing with the bank manager.

My parents started off with an L-shaped two-bedroom fibro flat-roofed house on a quarter acre of land in Leslie Road, Glenbrook, that ended up as a four-bedroom square flat-roofed house. At the back of the property was a tree that had an enormous choko vine growing over the top of it. Mum loved it – she saw it as a very cheap way to feed us green vegetables. The problem was she put choko into everything: stews, casseroles, served on the side with the standard meat and three veg and even tried to pass them off as apples in an apple crumble pie. To me chokos were the worst vegetable, and I became very good at scooping them into a handkerchief when mum wasn't watching and disposing of them in the toilet after dinner. One day I came up with the perfect plan to get rid of the chokos – I climbed the tree, picked every single choko off the vine and placed them into a box. I was planning to sell them on the highway but Mum would have gone ballistic if I had ventured there so I hauled the box to Mount Street, a main arterial road coming off the highway. It was about a kilometre from home and I set up a stall with a sign to sell them – three for 20 cents. I was amazed at two things, first that people actually wanted to buy chokos and second, just how quickly I was able to sell them. My business venture was very short lived. I don't think I had ever seen Mum so angry when she found out what I had done. It was so worth it, the chokos were gone for quite a long time. When they eventually grew back I made sure that I kept them to a bare minimum by just harvesting a few off the vine at a time. I was able to exchange a small handful with the owners of the local general store for some lollies.

My second not-so-good 'business venture' involved giving my brother 'financial advice'. He was one of those kids that constantly gave my parents heart failure, almost from the time he was born. He had a fascination with electrical sockets and was constantly jamming things into a socket and on a regular basis being jolted across the floor. As he grew older his fascination turned to the bulbs in the back of the TV. He was always willing to tinker with the TV to try and improve the picture quality. One day he was rummaging through the old TVs that were donated to St Vincent de Paul, looking for replacement bulbs that we could use in our TV. He came across a brown paper bag full of cash, about eight hundred dollars. This was

1975 and back then that amount of money was nearly two months' salary. A loaf of bread was 24 cents, a litre of milk was 30 cents and a newspaper was 12 cents.

My brother came to me and asked what he should do. I came up with the 'bright idea' of banking it in his school bank account – not foreseeing my parents' apoplexy if they saw that much money in his account. Back then we were encouraged to save and the Commonwealth Bank ran a school banking program where they would come to the school once a week and we could deposit some money into the account. At the time we were banking 20 cents a week. The local post office was also an agent for the bank and my plan was to go there with my brother, deposit the money and keep a little cash at home. Before we could put the plan into action my brother told a few of his mates that he had found this cash. Next thing he knew there were a bunch of kids that pounced on him and started bashing him up because they wanted him to give the cash to them. By the time he arrived home battered and bruised, the police had also arrived on the door step, presumably because the word had spread like wild fire. Mum was mortified, the police informed her that what we had done was stealing by finding. My brother and I confessed everything and handed the money over to the police. This was followed by an angry lecture from my parents that we should have told them about it and not taken matters into our own hands.

My schooling was at the local St Finbar's Catholic Primary School in Glenbrook. I later went to Caroline Chisholm Catholic Girls High School in Mulgoa – near Penrith. I couldn't wait until I could get a part time job and have an income. My first job was at the BP Emu Plains. It was a full service petrol station and my role was to fill the cars with petrol, wash the windscreen and check the tyre pressure. I also took on a job with Mr Whippy serving ice cream. I remember feeling great about having my own money. I started to do my HSC at Nepean High School. I had lots of fun but found I just didn't want to study anymore. The seniors at the school had a smoking room so we didn't have to use the toilets – the message about smoking being bad for your health hadn't taken hold back in 1979. I left towards the end of year eleven and started full time work as a clerk in the Rural Bank of New South Wales.

I spent 20 years at the Bank and for many years I kept wondering how one gets rich. Then one day in August 1998 I attended an unexpected event on property investing that changed my life. I share many of strategies and lessons that I learnt from this event in this book. I hope they will change your life like they did mine.

CHAPTER 2

Action Beats Inaction Every Single Time

Iron rusts from disuse; water loses its purity from stagnation...
even so does inaction sap the vigour of the mind.
Leonardo da Vinci

My brother-in-law Chris rang me one day in August 1998. He was really excited about having two tickets to a property investing event in Sydney to see a guy named John Burley who was presenting a very different real estate investment strategy. Chris couldn't find anyone to go with him and in fact it took me a while to warm to the idea of going to see someone speak on real estate investment. The strategy that was widely taught at the time was negative gearing. I had already had personal experience with negative gearing – a great strategy to lose money every single month whilst hoping and praying that the property will go up in value, at least enough to cover all the months and years of losses! As you have probably guessed by now, I am not a big fan of negative gearing.

I was also a young mum with two girls, four-year-old Laura and nine-month-old Courtney, so the idea of organising my husband Greg and children for me to have the day in Sydney seemed like way too much work. We were also living in Newcastle, two hours north of Sydney and it was a big deal even to travel down and back in the one day. Chris was really keen for me to go and then I had the thought that it would be really good to get out of the house as I had been feeling like I had a little bit of 'cabin fever'.

When I first heard John Burley speak on 'seller finance' as it is known in the USA ('vendor finance' in Australia), it made so much sense to me. Instead of having a property that would lose you money every single month, you could have properties that made you money every single month. You could also provide someone with a home opportunity that they may not have been able to access otherwise.

After I heard about this strategy I couldn't let it go. Nobody was doing this type of property investment in Australia at the time, although it was a strategy that had been used in Australia since the early days of our country's settlement right through to the 1950s and 1960s. In fact, my grandfather bought the land for his house on vendor finance back in the 1930s. Bank finance has really only started to assist home buyers since the middle of last century, although it is now the most common way of financing a home. To this day many people are locked out of home ownership even though they have affordability due to lack of a deposit or to a life event that may have impacted on their credit.

I wanted to learn more about it and that required me to go to the States (Phoenix, Arizona) to do the education. I had a couple of small issues that were preventing me from going. The first one was the course tuition fee, flights and accommodation and the second very important one was the care of the girls. When I first pitched the idea to my husband, well... you can imagine the response! "You want to take how much out of our savings and do what? Are you crazy?" After many loud discussions, my very wise husband suggested that if I wanted to do this course I should put one of these deals together to fund it and then he would be more than happy to take some time off work to look after the girls. He was thinking it would never happen and I was thinking about how soon I could make it happen. Amazingly, only one week after my husband set the challenge, an opportunity presented itself that would launch me into a fabulous career in vendor finance.

I was working part time at the State Bank of NSW. I constantly drove my colleagues insane with incessant jabbering about wanting to get involved in this niche of property investing. Friday evening rolls around and it is very common for people in the banking industry to have 'Friday night drinks' at the local pub. My opportunity presented itself when one of my colleagues asked me to tell him more about this real estate 'thing' I was involved with. He was recently divorced and he had come out of the divorce with literally just the shirt on his back. He was now in a new relationship but lacked the deposit to get into home ownership. He had the ability to afford the repayments, he just had no deposit. With a pen, a beer coaster and paper napkin

I drew up how he could get into a house of his own with me as his 'bank'. That weekend my colleague went out and found a house that would work with what we had discussed. He knew that I needed to make $10,000 from the deal. That amount, incidentally, was what I needed for my tuition, flights and accommodation.

This is how the deal worked:

- I negotiated the property down from $142,000 to $133,000.

- I raised a bank loan on the new property – my loan repayments were $930 per month.

- I sold the property to my colleague for $150,000. This sale price included all the purchasing and the profit of $10,000 that I wanted to make.

- My colleague's loan repayment back to me was $1,200 per month.

- This created a surplus cash flow for me of $270 per month.

- I was able to get a $10,000 credit card to fund my trip and tuition that cost me $144 per month in interest.

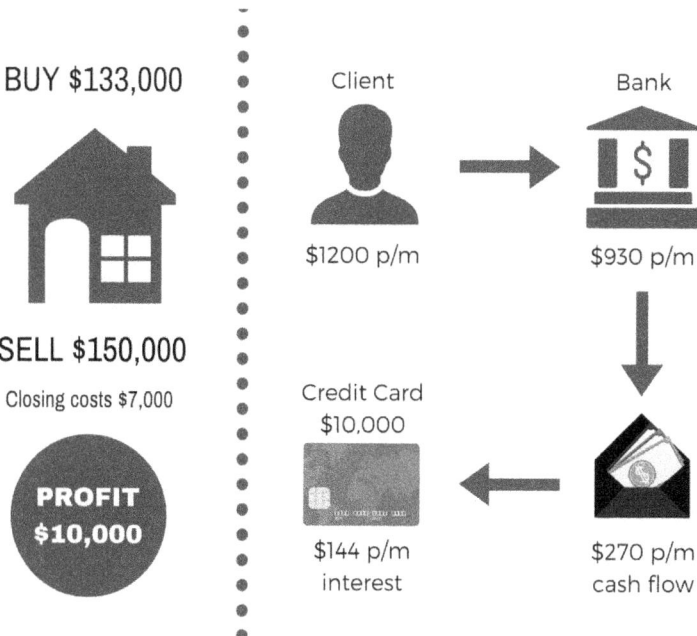

BUY $133,000

SELL $150,000

Closing costs $7,000

PROFIT $10,000

Client

$1200 p/m

Bank

$930 p/m

Credit Card $10,000

$144 p/m interest

$270 p/m cash flow

I now had the money for my trip and was beyond excited. I completed the course and came away with the big, hairy audacious goal to complete the acquisition of 10 properties and sell them on vendor finance. Never in my wildest dreams did I even consider that acquiring 151 properties would even be possible. Up to this stage of my life, I felt like I lived on the flat line of mediocrity, doing all the things that I was told were right, living a very ordinary life. I was completely unaware of or prepared for the wild roller coaster ride of a lifetime that has taught me so much about myself, other people and business. Wow, what a ride it has been.

SECTION 1: FOUNDATION

CHAPTER 3

Personal Financial Competence:
What Type Of Property Investor Are You?

Games are won by players who focus on the playing field – not by those whose eyes are glued to the scoreboard.

Warren Buffett

Seven levels of investor have been suggested by John Burley, a property investor who lives in Phoenix, Arizona. In my opinion, John has one of the greatest minds when it comes to property investment. John's teaching on the seven levels of investor and the money management strategies that I share with you in this chapter are among the most impactful things that I have ever heard. This knowledge has given me valuable perspective on money management and growing a large property portfolio.

If you have an opportunity, I would highly recommend attending a Burley Boot Camp in Arizona. Visit John's web site for details www. johnburley.com.

Level Zero: 'Non-Existent'

The **Non-Existent** investor technically speaking is not really an investor at all. This person is 'unconscious' when it comes to thinking about their financial situation. All they know is that they need money to survive and all they do is spend everything that they make. They give no thought to planning a future and tune out if the subject ever arises, as it is too painful for them to even contemplate. Their financial situation is so badly mismanaged that they don't qualify for even the simplest forms of credit. This is actually a good thing because they can't get themselves into too much trouble; they

are often in a better financial position than the person for whom credit is all too easily available.

Level One: 'Borrower'

The **Borrower** has a considerable amount of debt based around their consumption. They spend all that they make and then more. Consuming is what they know best. When they have money, it gets spent. At best, they 'survive' on a week-to-week basis, but mostly they consolidate their overspending on a credit card. Their answer to a money emergency is to take on more debt. The short-term consequences of this behaviour are that the problem is moved on to a credit card or wrapped up in another home loan refinance, increasing the repayments for consumer debt. The long-term consequences are that as more debt is added to existing debt, they then start to feel like they are drowning in debt.

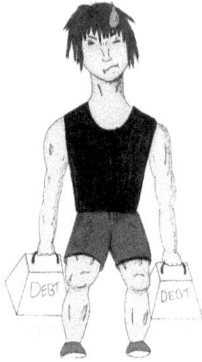

The Borrower's idea of 'financial planning' is to get a new Visa Card or MasterCard or to refinance their home in order to buy more things. When asked what they think the problem is, they invariably come to the conclusion that they just don't make enough money. If they just made more money, their financial situation would be fine. In fact, in many cases they are now 'starving' on what they only dreamed they could make five short years ago. The Borrower fails to see that the problem is not necessarily lack of income but rather their habits around money. They are often caught up in a vicious cycle of spiralling debt, coming to believe that their situation is hopeless, and as a result, giving up all hope. This person usually lives in complete financial denial.

The Borrower is often in a far worse financial position than the Non-Existent, because of the availability of credit although their potential for change may be greater. Surprisingly, not all people who in this category are low income earners; many are actually high income earners.

A very good friend of ours who stayed with us recently shared a story about his friend Jack who had spent many years working and living in Asia. Jack was a project engineer and ran huge projects, building big-name hotels throughout Asia. His annual salary was around $240,000. Whilst Jack was an awesome project engineer he had little knowledge about how money worked, and he certainly didn't know how to keep any of it. Over the years, Jack racked several hundreds of dollars on credit cards and serviced them at interest rates well over 20%. When one credit card blew out he either increased the limit or got another card. His plan was to make it through to retirement age of 65, retire on the pension and continue living in Asia because it is so much cheaper than living in Australia. Unfortunately, when his last contract finished he was only 61. Jack chewed through his accumulated superannuation within six months and now his wife is out working to meet the monthly living expenses.

I am not sure if Jack will be able to live on the pension even in Asia as he has never learnt to manage money. He is one of the lucky ones to be in a generation that has the safety net of the age pension to take care of him financially.

Level Two: 'Saver'

A **Saver** is the opposite of a Borrower. This person usually puts aside a small amount of money on a regular basis. The money is generally deposited into a low interest bank account. The Saver usually saves to consume rather than to invest (i.e. they save for a new TV, stereo, etc.). They are very afraid of financial matters and are unwilling to seek advice on finance. This type of person fears being in debt and doesn't seek help. Savers spend their time trying to save their pennies instead of learning how to invest. In times of inflation, they end up being the losers.

Level Three: 'Passive'

The **Passive** investor is also known as the 'level three screaming pig' for reasons shown below. These investors are aware of the need to invest, however choose the easy way out and do very little research.

Whilst they are intelligent people, when it comes to investing they are financially illiterate.

There are typically three categories of passive investor:

A. '**Gone into a Shell**'.

B. '**It Can't be Done.**'

C. The '**Victim**', also known as the '**Gambler**'.

A. The Gone into a Shell category is comprised of people who have convinced themselves that they don't understand money and never will. They make the following types of statements:

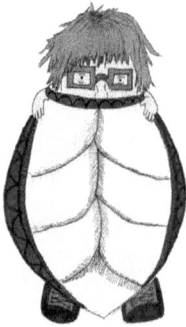

- "No one ever taught me what to do."

- "I'm just not very good with numbers."

- "I'll never understand how this investment works."

- "I'm just too busy to follow everything."

- "There's too much paperwork."

- "It's just too complicated."

- "I prefer to leave the money decisions to the professionals."

The excuses and justifications go on and on. All are designed to relieve them from having to take responsibility for their own money … and future. Due to their beliefs, they have very little idea where their money is invested or why. This type of investor blindly follows the market like a sheep and then squeals (a lot like a pig) before running to their own slaughter. Professional traders actually do commonly refer to this type of investor as 'pigs' because of this behaviour. Hence the 'level three screaming pig' mentioned earlier.

B. The It Can't Be Done passive investor has determined that all investments involving more than the most basic research by the investor and/or that promise much more than bank interest rates of return, are beyond them. They are cynical and an expert on why investing will not work. They are overwhelmed by cautiousness. They truly believe that high rates of return on investments are impossible, probably illegal or available only to the chosen few. They believe that the knowledge and skills required recognising such investments are beyond them in their present circumstances.

Their usual defence to demonstrations of successful investing by friends or high profile investors is that the investor knew something that they themselves couldn't possibly have known, or had an opportunity or available money that they themselves weren't given in order to make the investment so profitable.

It is common for these people to whine and complain about missing out on an investment opportunity (after the fact), as if some barrier other than their own psychology (in regards to investing) was to blame for them missing out. They are afraid and unwilling to gain the knowledge they need to invest successfully. They choose instead to 'shoot down' and criticise others in an attempt to make themselves, and their beliefs about investing, right.

C. The Victim / Gambler is the third category of passive investor. These investors have no principles or rules for investing. They impulsively buy high and (in a panic) sell low. They see the share market in the same way as they see a casino craps table. It's just luck. Throw the dice and hope.

The Victim passive investor is always looking for the holy grail, some get-rich-quick scheme that can solve all their financial woes. They are always searching for the 'secret' to investing outside of themselves, rather than within by changing their unsuccessful behaviour. They are not afraid of risk; in fact, they actually find risk exciting and often actively pursue it. They often fall for investment telemarketing schemes, direct mail opportunities and the 'hot' offerings in newspapers and magazines. They are quick to jump into initial public offerings (IPOs or floats); commodities and futures trading, mining, gold, gas, and oil stocks (and other low probability/high-risk mining ventures); ostrich farms; wine growing;

timber and tea tree plantations; and every other risky, trendy, exotic or 'tax-effective' investment known to mankind. They love to use 'sophisticated' investment techniques such as margins, short-sells, puts, calls, warrants and other options, without proper knowledge of exactly what it is they are committing to or the *real* investment risks.

These people are easily the worst investors on the planet. They are always trying to 'hit a home run' and they usually 'strike out' in a big way. When asked how they are doing, they will always state that they are "about even" or "a little bit up". The truth is that they have lost money.

Level 4: 'Automatic'

Automatic investors are clearly aware of the need to invest. However, unlike passive investors, they are actively involved in their investment decisions. They have a clearly laid out and written long-term plan that will enable them to reach their financial objectives. Automatic investors 'set' the flow of their finances so that they don't ever have to worry about money. They know that their mortgage is always paid; they know that their bills are taken care of; they have a charitable giving plan in place; they know that their wealth is accumulating because they took the time to set up the system to make sure all of this is done automatically with scheduled internet banking payments.

They are generally very conservative with well-balanced financial habits. They diligently spend time when it comes to learn about investing and make wise investment decisions. They understand the importance of debt elimination strategies; they live within their means and steadily increase their assets.

Level 5: 'Active' / 'Sophisticated'

This level of investor is an **Active** participant in the management of their investments. They consistently strive to optimise performance while minimising risk. Active investors are people who have a solid financial knowledge and are involved in more complex investment strategies. They have mastered and maintain the level four investor principals. They earn more than they spend. They are continuously seeking more information when it comes to investing. They have good money habits and a long track record of investment success. Active investors start small so they can learn the game first; they are always seeking to learn more and place a huge value on education. They create and structure their own deals, which generate extraordinary returns. They are focused on continuously growing their asset base and cash flow.

Level 6: 'Capitalist'

The **Capitalist** not only creates large amounts of wealth, they invariably also create vast legacies of innovation, efficiency, economic prosperity, employment opportunity and philanthropy, thereby greatly increasing the standards of living for hundreds of millions of people throughout the world every year.

Very few people are capable of reaching the Capitalist level, which represents investment excellence. They usually have large businesses and large investments. A true Capitalist creates investments and sells them to the market. They love the game of money and are generally very generous. They are the movers and shakers of the world economy by creating jobs and goods.

KEY POINTS

1. Being aware of the different levels of investors can help you hone in on where you want to be.

2. Aim to be a level four investor before a level five. If you don't, you won't have the correct foundation in place and will end up at level three.

3. Once people have mastered the level four investor principles, they start to experience financial freedom. Some like to accelerate the process by moving to level five.

4. Property investors are regarded as level five, active and sophisticated investors. Level five investors are people who have solid financial knowledge and are involved in more complex investment strategies. They have mastered and maintain the level four investor principles.

FELICITY'S INVESTING TIP

Aim to be a level four automatic investor. This is the level where you have the systems in place and you know exactly what your money is doing. Level four is the launch pad to financial freedom.

CHAPTER 4

Set Up Your Finances On Auto Pilot:
The Automatic Money System

*Budget your expenses so that you may have money to pay for your necessities,
to pay for your enjoyments and to gratify your worthwhile desires without
spending more than nine-tenths of your earnings.*

George S. Clason

This chapter goes into depth on how to establish yourself as a level four investor. I believe the inspiration for 'the automatic money system' came from the book, *The Richest Man in Babylon* by George S. Clason. The book has become an inspirational classic to millions of readers, despite being set thousands of years ago in the historical city of Babylon. The stories and principles seem just as applicable today as they did in ancient times.

When I first learnt about managing money from my parents, we were taught to pay the bills first and then put a small amount of money into our savings for a rainy day. The roof over our head was always paid for even before food went into our mouths. Any form of extravagance was frowned upon. This attitude came from a time when my parents experienced life after the great depression and World War II, when even the basics were difficult to come by. My parents' attitude towards money was tough and came from challenging times. The automatic money system means feeling not poor but empowered to enjoy life whilst being a good steward of money.

The first time I heard John Burley talk about the automatic system, I felt like the pennies had dropped and filled all the missing gaps in what I thought I knew about finances. It literally turned my world upside down and made saving and investing the top priority. The idea highlighted just how much money slips through your fingers unconsciously. Having a system to follow took the stress away from managing money because you save first and only spend what is left over. It left me with head space to become creative about making my money go further rather than stressed about how I was going to pay the bills. I wanted my kids to understand this system too and right from the time they started school, they were given an allowance of $5. They had three money boxes, one for saving, one for charity and one for their spending money. The system worked so well that when they grew older the money boxes were replaced with bank accounts and the system continues to this day.

Case Study – Maggs

A very good friend, Maggs, was stressing badly about her finances. She is an amazing women raising two adopted Cambodian children on a single wage. We sat down one night over a glass of wine and spoke about how to implement the system. With renewed energy and able to see the light at the end of the tunnel, Maggs went about setting up the system in the following days. She set up automatic fortnightly payments to her savings account and fortnightly payments for literally every bill that she had or was likely to have. To her delight, she could also contribute to her favourite charities and she took to debt elimination as if it was a national sport! She even set up her own kids with their own bank accounts so they could apply the system to their allowances.

AUTOMATED MONEY SYSTEM

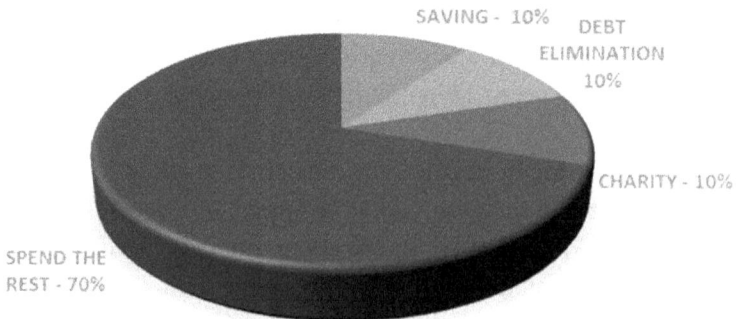

SAVING - 10%   DEBT ELIMINATION 10%

CHARITY - 10%

SPEND THE REST - 70%

I have shared this system with many of my clients, and many people have the same feeling of relief and a sense of wellbeing when the system is implemented. I can promise you if you take the time to implement the system you are well and truly on the way to financial freedom.

Step One – Pay yourself first. Whether you are paid weekly, fortnightly or monthly, 10% of your pay is calculated and set to come automatically out of your salary or everyday bank account into a separate savings or investment account. This is the money you will not spend but *keep for your future wellbeing*. Without too much effort you should be able to stop spending 100% of your income.

Get your boss or bank to direct debit this money automatically when you get paid. That way you won't see it, you won't have to do it manually and it won't be painful. Why do you think the tax office takes their money before you get it? Because they are guaranteed to get it that way! Imagine if we had to pay our taxes manually ourselves every pay day, the country would go broke pretty quick.

An important tip – make sure you *separate* your savings from your everyday account. All too often I see people who start the habit but don't separate the savings. What ends up happening is that they are never too sure about what is savings and what they can spend. This is even more important if you are saving the deposit for your first home and your deposit amount is likely to be less than 20% of the purchase price. The bank will want to see at least 5% of the amount in the bank account as 'genuine savings'. The other very practical reason is that generally speaking; you are less likely to 'dip' into your savings if they are in a separate account.

Step Two – Put an additional 10% towards eliminating any existing debt. In the next chapter we go into depth on how you can eliminate debt very quickly and efficiently.

Step Three – Give 10% to charity. The question around charity invariably gets raised and the most common reaction to paying 10% from your hard earned money to charity is "Why?" My husband's reaction was, "Are you kidding me? We don't have money to give to charity! The only charity that I know that needs money is the Greg Heffernan charity!" However, when we looked at the reason for giving to charity we realised it is part of the responsibility and reciprocity associated with creating wealth and being a good steward of that wealth.

You often hear the saying that the more you give, the more you receive, and this true in many cases. Giving to charity simply brings you more wealth, not that you do it for that reason. Furthermore, you may never know what indirect benefits giving to charity may provide you.

If you look at many of the successful entrepreneurs today, just about all of them have a program that gives back to the community or a cause that is close to their heart.

When I started researching for this book I asked many of my successful property investor clients what they were seeking when they first started out and what they continued to seek as they built their portfolios. In every single case, they sought financial freedom initially and then as they became more successful, they discovered they were looking for fulfilment and that this translated into being able to give back in some way.

Step Four - Spend the 70%. I think most of us can do this step without much encouragement! From personal experience with the automated money system I find it is easier to set it up with smaller percentages to start with just to get the habit underway. I have introduced the system to a number of clients who are trying to save for their first home. Many of them start with a small amount such as $50 per week and gradually increase the amount until they meet the desired level of 10% of their income.

I am going to digress a little now and talk about living expenses. If you find that applying the above formula to your current income leaves you short on your current expenses, it could be an indication that you are living outside your means.

There has been a strong focus from ASIC (Australia Securities Investment Commission) for lenders to step up and make reasonable enquiries into living expenses. Traditionally banks used benchmarks for people's living expenses and did not make any enquiry into an individual's actual expenses. If you apply for a loan now you will be required to disclose to the bank what your living expenses are. This is then compared to the benchmarks that the banks have in their servicing calculators. Many Australian banks use the Household Expenditure Measurement (HEM) from the Australian Bureau of Statistics (ABS) as the benchmark for comparison with disclosed living expenses.

This is how the Melbourne Institute of Applied Economic and Social Research describes the HEM:

> *The Household Expenditure Measure (HEM) is a measure that reflects a modest level of household expenditure for various types of families. The first HEM was produced for 2011 Q1. Since then there have been quarterly updates, with a major change being the 2011 Q3 update when the 2009/10 Household Expenditure Survey (HES) was used for the first time.*
>
> *To produce the HEM, all 600+ expenditure items in the HES are classified as absolute basics, discretionary basics or non-basics. The HEM is taken as the median spend on absolute basics plus the 25th percentile spend on discretionary basics. A rough idea of this classification is that absolute basics captures almost all food, children's clothing, utilities, transport costs, and communications. Discretionary basics include take away food, restaurants, confectionary, alcohol and tobacco, adult clothing, childcare, and entertainment. Examples of non-basics are luxury services (e.g. gardeners) and overseas holidays. Rents and mortgage payments aren't included by design, as the HEM is meant to be a net-of-housing costs measure. Every quarter the HEM is updated using state-specific values for each of the 90 or so CPI minor groups.*

I have been careful not to use the six-letter swear word, 'BUDGET', however it is *really, really* worth sitting down and getting a handle on what you are actually spending. This will also put you on the path of financial freedom. When I have my mortgage broker hat on. I see many people's financial position each day. I hear a lot of moaning and groaning about filling out the living expenses – it seems to be in the same category as eating well and doing exercise. But if you don't focus on this area, you are more likely to have poor financial health. A really compelling reason to do so is that it will serve you well and improve your financial position dramatically. If you spend just one hour month per month paying attention to your finances, your chances of financial freedom are increased exponentially.

There are many great tools and apps for doing the job. I have a calculator on my website that can assist you with the job. Go to www.propertyloanadvisor.com.au/budget-planner.

If you are a paper-and-pen person, try the following monthly expenses template – by the way, it will come in handy when you go to the bank to borrow, because they will ask for it. More importantly, it will keep you honest about what you do spend and give you a place to start to trim if you are overspending.

MONTHLY LIVING EXPENSES

Residential	MONTHLY AMOUNT
Rent	$
Home Loan Payments	$
Personal Loan Payments	$
Credit Card Payments	$
Rates / Body Corporate Fees	$
Gas, Electricity, Water	$
Telephone, Mobiles, Internet	$
House & Contents Insurance	$
Transport	
Vehicle Lease Payments	$
Vehicle Registration & Insurance	$
Petrol & Parking	$
Public Transport	$
Medical	
Doctor / Specialists	$
Medication	$
Health Insurance	$
Personal	
Food & Groceries	$
Lunches / Take Aways	$
Shoes & Clothing	$

Sport & Entertainment	$
Pay TV	$
Birthdays & Christmas Gifts	$
Pet Costs	$
Other – Please Specify	$
Educational/ Children	
School Fees	$
School Excursions	$
Classes	$
Child Care	$
Child Support Payments	$
Uniform / Clothing	$
Other	
	$
	$
Total Monthly Living Expenses	**$**

Step Five - lead a debt avoidance lifestyle. This step is the one that will keep you from getting into chronic debt in the first place. It is also at this step that we look at the difference between 'good debt' and 'bad debt'. Bad debt is usually an impulse buy that ends up on your credit card. How many times have you seen an ad for something that you never knew existed until that very moment and decided right there and then that you must absolutely have the item right now? And how many of those items have ended up in the garage or on the nature strip with a 'Free to good home' sign or donated to the Salvos? Everyone laughs but how true is it? Just having the awareness that this actually happens to most human beings is usually enough to correct the behaviour. There are a few hardcore people with an addiction to spending, it is true, but that is more about them buying something to make them feel better. Good debt, on the other hand, is leverage. This is where you borrow money to purchase an investment property, for example. I cover this in greater depth in the Chapter 7 – Finance is Leverage.

The great thing about the automatic money system is that you can't spend what you don't have. If you are committed to the program, you find ways of being creative to give your money better buying power. One of my wonderful friends, Kerrie, has every imaginable coupon book under the sun for restaurants, travel, groceries and clothing. Kerrie doesn't go without anything, in fact by the way she lives you would think she was a millionaire many times over. Kerrie sources the most amazing luxury travel discounts that I have ever seen. Kerrie's motto is, "If it ain't discounted I ain't buying".

Whilst the automatic money system formula is very simple, the sad fact is that most people cannot live on 70% of what they make. Sadly, most people in the western world (particularly Australia, the United States, United Kingdom and most of Europe) spend more than they earn. The extra spending generally ends up as a credit card debt.

Often the solution that most people come to is that they have to make more money. They invariably start looking for a job that pays more and usually trade far more of their time for it. However, they never really stop and think about the underlying problem. The underlying problem is that they are spending more than they are making. People get caught up in the 'I need to make more money' trap and this becomes a never-ending cycle. They make more money and then spend more money, often more than before.

The fact is that the size of your income actually has very little to do with your ability to obtain financial freedom. The truth is this: it is not what you make that matters, but rather what you keep and what you do with it. Your biggest mistake would be to get hung up on your income.

The concept of living on 70% of your income is a shift in your belief system. And guess what … if you believe it can't be done you are right.

If you are really struggling and drowning in debt, try the strategies in the next chapter to first get yourself out of debt and then implement the automatic money system.

KEY POINTS

1. Level four investors have mastered the automatic money system.

2. Having a system takes the stress out of managing money.

3. Step one – Pay 10% to yourself first as savings.

4. Step two – Put 10% towards eliminating any existing debt.

5. Step three – Give 10% to charity

6. Step four – Spend the 70%.

7. Step five – lead a debt avoidance lifestyle.

8. Set up separate accounts for saving – make sure you *separate* your savings from your everyday account.

9. Making more money will not solve financial problems. It is not about how much you make, it is all about how much you keep.

FELICITY'S INVESTING TIP

Action the automatic money system as quickly as you can. Mastering it will give you a strong foundation for property investment.

CHAPTER 5

Become Completely Debt Free Using My 7-Step Debt Elimination Plan

Debt, n. An ingenious substitute for the chain and whip of the slavedriver.
Ambrose Bierce

Debt is the modern day equivalent of slavery and bondage. It keeps people in jobs that they hate and often in a downward spiral of ever-increasing debt. Many people continue to spend not because they need anything but because it is a drug and helps them feel better about their lives, keeping them in the never-ending cycle of hating their job, spending to feel better and ending up in more debt.

When you are using equity from your home to buy investment property you should also have a debt elimination strategy on all your personal debt. Ideally the goal should be to have the roof over your head completely debt free. Building a property portfolio will require capital or equity from your home, and as long as you have a strategy to pay down the portion of the debt that is not used for investment you are well on your way to achieving that goal especially if you apply the strategy in this chapter.

Case Study – Mayo

Virginia (aka Mayo) was deeply in debt with no hope of retiring. Mayo is a delightful lady with a huge heart. She works full-time and is also a foster carer for several disadvantaged children. I first met Mayo a few years ago when she approached me to refinance her home loan and see if we could wrap all her small debt to help her manage the monthly payments better. This type of scenario always poses the question of whether it is the right thing for a client to wrap up the debt and extend the term out to 30 years again. To do so in Mayo's case would have done her a huge disservice.

Mayo had ten separate loans, most of which were small with huge monthly repayments by comparison. The first thing most people want to do is just wrap it up in their home loan just to stop the noise. (Have you ever noticed just how much squeaky loud noise comes from a small debt?) Well poor old Mayo had so much noise from her debts that it kept her up at night. She felt so overwhelmed that she tried paying extra on all her debts in the hope that she could repay them faster. The problem was, she had no system in place, and she would often pay too much out every month, then run short for basic items. She would then use the credit cards again, and this was keeping her in the continuing downward spiral of accumulating debt. And this was happening despite her annual income of $115,000.

Wrapping the debt up into the home was not going to be the financially responsible thing to do either because the real problem was her money habits. At the time, Mayo was a single parent aged 59, earning really good income but with the dreadful habit of not being able to say No. If she wanted something, she put it on a credit card. If her large extended family wanted money, she gave them money. I suggested to Mayo that we put together a debt elimination plan that included some coaching on how to say No. In fact, I made it really easy for her to say no, simply by asking her to carry very little money and put other disposable income in a bank account that required some effort to access. Mayo was very compliant and did everything I suggested.

7-Step Debt Elimination Plan

1. List all income sources.

2. List all loans and credit cards.

3. List for each debt: who it is owed to, the total amount owed and the minimum monthly payment.

4. Calculate the payment to debt ratio, also known as the 'payoff rate'. This is calculated by dividing the present amount owed by the minimum monthly payment. For example, if the total amount owed is $5000 and the current minimum monthly payment for that loan is $400, you get a ratio of 12.5 by dividing the former by the latter. 5. Rank each debt from the smallest ratio to the largest. This shows your payment priority, the debt with the smallest ratio being your top priority and the debt with the largest ratio being your last priority.

6. Add at least an additional 10% to your debt repayments.

7. Cut up all credit cards

Mayo's 7-Step Debt Elimination Plan

Following **step 1**, we first collated Mayo's income sources:

• Wages $1700 f/n

• Family Payment $417 f/n

• Foster care Payment $2300 f/n

• Total earned monthly $9570 (Annually $114,842)

The following table shows **steps 2 to 5** for Mayo:

	Creditor Name	Amount Balance	Minimum Payment	Payoff Ratio	Payoff Priority
1	Home Loan	$225,000.00	$1517.00	148	10
2	Car Loan # 1	$9,648.00	$620.00	16	4
3	Car loan # 2	$33,251.00	$722.00	46	9
4	GE Credit line	$1,500.00	$130.00	12	2
5	CUA Credit Card	$3,500.00	$105.00	34	7
6	Myer Visa	$3,000.00	$90.00	34	8
7	ANZ Credit Card	$6,500.00	$210.00	31	5
8	Rent smart 1	$3,407.00	$285.00	12	1
9	Rent smart 2	$5,644.00	$146.00	38	6
10	Cash first	$2500.00	$152.00	16	3
	Balance Total	**$293,950.00**	**$3977.00**		

Mayo's payoff ratio (column 5) was calculated on each debt in order to work out the priority (column 6) in which to pay them off.

I suggested that Mayo make minimum repayments on all her debts except the one that was priority number 1, the Rent Smart 1 debt of $3,407.

Step 6 suggests that you add at least 10% to your debt repayments and Mayo chose to pay an extra $250 each month. In other words, for the Rent Smart 1 debt, she paid the minimum payment of $285 plus $250 for debt elimination, making a total of $535 per month. This debt was repaid within 7 months.

Mayo then applied the amount of $535 to the second priority debt, GE Credit Line. Its minimum payment was $130 per month, making a total monthly repayment of $665. Mayo paid this debt off in 2 months. She continued in this way, extinguishing one debt after another.

Following **Step 7**, Mayo nervously cut up all her credit cards. She had become very dependent on them because they had 'come to the rescue' on so many occasions when she ran out of money.

I calculated the time it would take if Mayo consistently paid the additional $250 per month and did not use her credit cards or take out any further short term debt, she would have every debt including her home loan, car loans, credit cards, and personal loans repaid in 7 years and 9 months. Mayo was astounded – NO WAY, she said in her raspy voice that is not possible. I did remind her that she had now committed $4227 of her income for the next 7 years and 9 months to completely repaying all her debts.

In 2 years and 7 months Mayo had paid off all the credit cards and car loans and was only left with the home loan. Mayo is highly motivated and is now well ahead with the plan on her home loan. And she is feeling really good about her retirement.

Mayo is like many Australians and people in countries like Canada, US, UK, Europe and New Zealand. Australians are the not-so-proud owners $32 billion worth of credit card debt. That is an average of $4,300 per card holder according to the ASIC Money Smart website. The interest bill is a ridiculous $5.3 billion annually. This statistic, echoed in other first world countries, keeps too many people impoverished. Their lives would be greatly improved by something as simple as financial education.

I have shared this system with many clients when they go to refinance in order to get equity from their properties to purchase a future investment property. One of the most memorable is Mick.

Case Study – Mick

Mick took to the system like a duck to water. He had never really thought too much about what he spent, and if he ever needed anything he just went out and made more money. In fact, he had gone through life without much financial education, he just knew how to earn money. When we first met, he had the usual credit cards and personal loans as well as all the common household bills that seem to turn up for payment at the most inconvenient time. Mick was very inspired by Mayo's story and thought he would test the system for himself.

Mick immediately got into action and started to collate his debts. He then made a list of all his regular household bills. Every few weeks I received a text message and photo of a loan that was paid out or a bill that was paid in advance. Mick was so excited about the system that he decided to pay everything daily. I explained that it wasn't necessary to pay daily and that weekly would work just as well and was probably more efficient. He remains convinced that paying daily works for him and who I am I to stand in the way of someone obliterating their debts? He has now modified the system and calls it the '$5-a-day empire'!

A word on bankruptcy

All too often I see clients who have declared bankruptcy because they were weighted down with debt and wanted the problem to go away. When I asked why did you go bankrupt most people's response was I just needed the phone calls from the creditors to stop. Declaring bankruptcy will make the phone calls stop but it will also severely impact the way that you live in the future. A trustee in bankruptcy will step into your shoes to do the following:

- sell your assets, including those you acquire or become entitled to during your bankruptcy (although you will be able to keep certain types of assets)

- recover any income you earn over a certain limit

- investigate your financial affairs and may in certain circumstances recover property that you have transferred to someone else prior to your bankruptcy.

According to the Australian Financial Security Authority website the top three reasons for declaring bankruptcy was:

1. Unemployment or loss of income

2. Excessive use of credit

3. Domestic discord or relationship breakdown

If you have been impacted from a life event like loss of job or relationship breakdown, the best thing to do is contact each creditor and make an arrangement to pay a reduced amount, this will make the phone calls stop. Make sure you do a proper budget and use the debt elimination strategy above, only agree to pay what you can afford to pay not what the creditor thinks you should pay. There are hardship laws in place in Australia and anyone dealing in credit has to abide by them. There are also many companies now that will mediate with your creditors on your behalf if you don't want to do it yourself.

The problem with declaring bankruptcy is that whilst you may only be in bankruptcy for three years and have the record on your credit report for seven years, the bankruptcy record stays with you for life. It can dramatically impact your ability to borrow in the future, which means banks may request higher deposits and /or charge you a higher interest rate. I am not saying never declare bankruptcy, I am saying, get the right advice before you do. Implementing a debt elimination strategy is a really good way to get back in control of your finances and avoid bankruptcy.

KEY POINTS

1. When you are using equity from your home to buy investment property you should also have a debt elimination strategy on all your personal debt.

2. The seven steps in a debt elimination plan:

Step One.   List all income sources.

Step Two.   List all loans and credit cards.

Step Three. List who each debt is owed to, the total amount that is owed and the minimum monthly payment for that debt.

Step Four. Calculate the payment to debt ratio by dividing the debt owing by the minimum repayment.

Step Five. Rank each debt according to payment to debt ratio. The debt with the smallest ratio should be paid off first, and the debt with the largest ratio should be paid off last.

Step Six.   Add at least 10% to your debt repayments.

Step Seven. Cut up all credit cards

FELICITY'S INVESTING TIP

Learn the difference between 'good debt' and 'bad debt'. Good debt includes loans to purchase assets that go up in value, such as an investment property. Bad debt includes loans for the purchase of assets that go down in value, such as a car loan, personal loans and credit cards. Extinguish bad debt as quickly as you can.

CHAPTER 6

What is your Niche?

Identify your niche and dominate it. And when I say dominate, I just mean work harder than anyone else could possibly work at it.

Nate Parker

To have a property niche is to specialise on a particular type of property investment that will normally relate to a specific opportunity you've noticed or doing business in a way that particularly suits your skills. For example, buying property to improve requires a particular skill set: knowledge and abilities in renovation.

There are three main benefits to niching:

1. **Stay focused.** Many investors get excited about every available deal, which often creates a mental traffic jam and leads to procrastination.

2. **Save time**. Instead of looking at every property deal as a potential purchase and spending time analysing each one, the deals that don't fit into your niche can be discounted at a glance. After a certain number of deals you know exactly what works and what does not work.

3. **Become the go-to person**. When you are known for a specific niche, real estate agents or other investors will contact you first about a deal. The deals that you want come to you rather than you having to track them.

The really important thing to remember about property investment is to get clarity around a niche. There are different strategies for different niches, and no one size fits all. If you have no clarity around your niche, it will cause confusion and poor results. I have seen investors trying to combine strategies in the hope of

ร

supercharging their returns, however it can turn into disaster because there is too much expectation as to what result is expected for the property.

The Capital Growth Niche

A buyer who invests for capital growth hopes that over time the property will be worth more than what it was purchased for.

Capital growth largely depends on where you buy and what you buy. Major cities tend to show the most growth. The yield or rental return needs to be taken into account. In many cases, for a property to get capital growth it will be at the expense of the cash flow. In other words, the property is likely to cost you money every single month until the rent rises enough to cover the outgoings or until the property is sold to collect the capital gain.

Many investors looking for capital growth expect a property to double in price every 7 to 10 years. But this purely depends on supply and demand, which is why major cities tend to see the best capital growth. However, even this is not always a given. If you look at the major cities around Australia (and the world), many of them have a positive net migration rate. This means that more people are entering than leaving, which increases the demand for housing.

Many investors research population growth, infrastructure for schools, shopping and transport, and the median house price when looking for a property with good growth potential. The median house price is the halfway point of all houses sold in a period of time. For example, if 101 houses sell in a 3-month period, the median house price is the one in the middle of a numerically sorted list of all 101 prices. In this case, the median price will have 50 house prices above it and 50 below it in the list.

The median house prices differs from the mean (or average) price, which is found by adding the sold prices together and then dividing this by the number of sales. The median price is used rather than the mean because it is a more accurate indicator of the market, as it reflects the sample size being used.

Using the median price can be a problem if a large number of particularly expensive or less expensive homes have been sold in a given period. In these circumstances, you will often notice large differences in the median price of a certain area from month to month. For this reason, it is better to view median prices over periods of time and monitor the trends, rather than to look at one month's figures in isolation. Viewing the median house price over a long period of time will show the trends of capital growth.

The tables below show that the June 2015 median house prices in Australian cities were a far cry from the median house prices in 1995. People always wonder why they didn't buy more houses back in 1995 and the reason is affordability. If you had had affordability back in 1995, you probably would have bought more houses. In today's terms, how many $1 million houses can you support now? The answer is probably only one, and that is if you are lucky. The next question is, what is the likelihood of a $1 million property in Sydney being worth $2 million in 10 years time? Who knows? Maybe we will all look back enviously at the current million dollar Sydney house price.

2015 June Quarter median house prices

City	Median house price $
Sydney	$1,000,616.00
Melbourne	$668,030.00
Darwin	$654,270.00
Canberra	$616,313.00
Perth	$605,089.00
Brisbane	$490,855.00
Adelaide	$479,285.00
Hobart	$325,972.00
National	$701,827.00

Source: Domain

Median House prices in 1995

City	Median house price $
Sydney	$196,750

Melbourne	$129,000
Darwin	$165,375
Canberra	$155,550
Perth	$126,788
Brisbane	$147,000
Adelaide	$111,500
Hobart	$106,750
National	$142,339

Source: HOUSING PRICES IN AUSTRALIA: 1970 TO 2003 Peter Abelson and Demi Chung

It is easy to believe that the Sydney median house price of $1 million is an isolated event, however a quick sweep around the globe and you find that median house prices have escalated in many other major cities too. This reflects population growth, affordability and demand for property in these cities.

Median House prices in global cities in 2015

City	Median house price $
Auckland	NZ$705,236
New York	US$1,250,000
London	BP£456,229
Vancouver	C$922,000
San Francisco	US$1,105,000

The big thing to remember about capital growth strategy is that whilst the growth prices may look impressive, you still have to be able to afford to hold them. To hold on to a property whilst it bleeds your account every month for many years is no fun. It is a huge commitment and a major risk to enter into a transaction like that.

The Cash Flow Niche

A buyer in the cash flow niche hopes that their property will yield higher rental returns versus the capital used to acquire the property.

These properties tend to be in regional areas, however there are pitfalls if you buy in the wrong area. Again, it comes down to market research. Larger regional areas with sizeable populations and plenty of diverse industry (that is, not reliant on a single industry) provide good opportunities for the cash flow strategies.

Set and forget

Many investors love the 'set and forget' of a cash flow property. They never have to worry about meeting constant monthly negative cash flow. They simply acquire a property that meets their criteria and have the tenant pay off the mortgage. They employ a good property manager to oversee the property and have regular rent reviews to make sure that the property keeps pace with the market rent. Every so often they do a small cosmetic renovation that keeps the property looking smart and also increases their ability to increase the rent. More often than not, they pick up a small capital gain but this is a bonus and never included in the calculation.

Investors in this niche acquire multiple properties because they are affordable, having completed research and risk assessment to ensure the properties are purchased on numbers and not emotion. Investors make sure when they are acquiring properties that the rent will cover the mortgage, rates, insurance, property management and some. Many will look to fix their interest rates so that they can predict their return.

Buyer beware

There are classic examples of chasing property purely on rental return. For example, many investors went to mining towns during the boom and loaded up on property. The problem was that when the mining boom ended, so did the rent returns as well as the ability to sell the properties. It was great whilst it lasted, but many of these investors now have huge headaches: they have had to drop the rent significantly in order to keep tenants, to the point where the properties now have negative cash flow. They are bleeding cash every single month with very little ability to get out of the situation. Selling is not an option because nobody wants to buy now that the mine has closed. The big lesson here is to do your research. There are plenty of very good moderate cash flowing properties in large population areas with diverse industry.

Cash buys in small towns

I know investors in this niche who focus on cash buys in small towns to get the high rental returns. They are cash buys because most lenders probably won't lend in these towns and if they do, the funding is often restricted. That been said, these towns often have a small infrastructure and people moving there for the country lifestyle will always need rental accommodation. The downside to buying in small towns is that it is not quick to sell the property. On the other hand, if you are not in a hurry to sell and are content to have your cash invested in the property for the rental return, they can provide a decent cash flow.

Commercial vs residential

Many people look at commercial property because the returns are higher than on a residential property. A commercial building purchase is quite different to a residential property purchase. When purchasing a residential property, a bank will take into consideration the rent potential of the property but it does not necessarily have to be performing as a rental property when purchased. Conversely, a commercial property needs to have a lease agreement in place in order for the bank to take into consideration its earning potential. If a commercial property is vacant, it is likely the bank will assume a zero return for the purpose of their serviceability calculators. This is because there are many commercial properties vacant in every city and town and the banks see a vacant building as a risk. The only time rent is taken into consideration is when the business will be the owner occupier of the commercial building. When looking at commercial properties for investment, make enquiries about the tenant(s). The longer and more stable the lease, the more favourably the bank will view the proposition.

Vendor finance – another cash flow strategy

Vendor finance is giving someone an opportunity to own a home as opposed to renting a home. The cash flow from the property is usually more than the rental return on the same property because people are happy to pay more for a home ownership opportunity. Vendor finance works best when the property is acquired below market value and then on-sold at a little above market value. For example, if the property is worth $400,000, you may be able to acquire it at $370,000 and on-sell on vendor finance for $420,000. Let's say your loan repayments are $2100 per month and the potential vendor finance purchaser's payments are $3900 per month, the cash flow to you is $900 per month.

With vendor finance there are several ways that your transaction makes money. The first is the deposit paid upfront at the beginning of the transaction, the second is the monthly cash flow and the third is the capital gain at the end of the transaction, unless the transaction runs the full term of say 30 years, in which case you pick up cash flow for 30 years.

Vendor finance is an advanced strategy and if you are running a vendor finance business you will need to have an Australian Credit Licence and a real estate licence. Even within the vendor finance niche there are different ways to do a vendor finance transaction. The three main ways are:

1. **Selling the property with an instalment contract** – This is similar to a loan contract where the loan amount, term (usually 30 years), interest rate and repayment amount are noted. I am a little biased as I believe this is the best way to vendor finance.

2. **Selling the property on a lease with an option to purchase** – known as 'rent-to-buy' in Australia or 'rent-to-own' in the United States and Canada, this is where the first contract is a standard residential tenancy lease agreement and the second is the option to purchase the property. This contract includes the option fee, the time that the potential purchaser has to take the option up and any rent credits that may apply if the potential purchaser takes up the option. These contracts are relatively short, ranging from 12 months to three years. There has been a tendency to abuse the intention of giving someone a home ownership opportunity,

if the potential buyer cannot get bank finance at the end of the option period and the owner of the property doesn't extent the option, the potential purchaser can lose all the money paid under the option agreement. I am not a big fan of this style of contract unless there is also an agreement that if bank finance is not obtainable then an instalment contract will be offered.

3. **Second mortgage carry back** – sometimes known as deposit finance, this is where the potential buyer is able to raise some of the money from the bank, usually 80% of the value of the property on a first mortgage, and the vendor carries back 20% on a second mortgage.

The six main steps in the vendor finance process are:

1. **Acquisition** – being able to acquire property below market value is the number one priority. The best types of property are the ones that are 20% below the median price range in suburban areas. They are where the everyday person lives, in areas where they can feel safe and raise a family. The houses are usually a couple of rungs up from the bottom of the price range.

2. **Marketing** – the main priority here is to on-sell the acquired property for an affordable price. If you did the acquisition step correctly this shouldn't be a problem. People in this country understand weekly repayments, so when presenting all the information on the property to the buyer it is a good idea to quote the weekly repayments as this gives people an idea of how it compares with a weekly rent payment and they are also able to quickly identify if it can fit in their budget. There are strict rules around how to advertise on the various media platforms, such as not quoting interest rates without noting the comparison rate and not quoting repayment amounts – this information is covered when the buyer makes an enquiry.

3. **Qualifying the potential buyers** – The main objective here is that you want someone that can see the transaction through to whenever they get bank finance to complete the purchase. The people that should not be accepted are the ones that are classed as vulnerable, that is they are on social security or low incomes. An exit strategy should be done for each potential client to work out when the likelihood of them being able to complete the purchase with bank finance down the track. Most vendor finance deals run for five to seven years. You do have to be prepared to go longer at times.

4. **Preparation of the paperwork** – The main objective is to have a solicitor draw up the contract and liaise with the purchaser's solicitor to ensure everything is in place before your buyer takes possession. It is at this point the buyer is issued with information on the property, including the sale price and the terms of the agreement. A deposit is usually collected at this point.

5. **Handing over possession** – the inspection phase is particularly important when handing over possession under a rent-to-buy situation. A condition report needs to be completed. The potential buyer is handed the keys and the repayment terms are reiterated, and direct debits are established to collect the payments.

6. **Managing the property** – This involves preparing statements for the buyers and ensuring that the repayments are made on time. From time to time you do have to manage an arrears situation where certain procedures must be followed depending on what contract you are using. Regardless of the contract, action has to be taken quickly and you have to be assertive – the motto here is soft on the person but hard on the situation.

The above is a brief overview of vendor finance. It does require some serious training, and as I write this book, I am also looking forward to the availability of a Certificate IV in vendor finance in the future for those wishing to pursue it as a business.

The Renovation Niche

Like the others, this niche requires a high degree of market research. To renovate you also have to have reasonable knowledge on many trades such as carpentry, electrical, plumbing, tiling and painting to name a few. Some of the trades such as electrical and plumbing will require a licenced trades person to do the work. The key to making money in this niche is to be highly organised with all your resources. The great renovators have excellent acquisition skills; they know that they have to acquire the property below market because that is where their profit is, and that a good renovation will enhance their profit. The renovator's budgeting skills have been highly honed and once the game plan for the renovation is mapped out, they must have the ability not to let emotions kick in and change the original plan.

The renovator has to be able to raise finance to acquire a property either through traditional means such as a bank or through joint ventures with other investors. Raising money through a bank can pose problems as the renovator's income is similar to the property developer's income in that the pay check usually arrives when the property is sold. This is why many people do the property renovation niche as a weekend warrior. They need their nine-to-five job to qualify for bank finance which means they only have the weekends to do the project.

Case Study – Connie and Marc

My renovator clients Connie and Marc do this niche particularly well and have made a great business from renovating. They map their whole year out to work on eight to nine projects in total, that is a renovation project every five to six weeks. They transform really ugly houses into beautiful masterpieces. They have a team of trades people for the work that require a licenced trades person to perform and they do all of the other work themselves. They have been known to have completely renovated a bathroom for $900 where most people would have estimated that it cost somewhere between $15,000 to $20,000. They are highly skilled in staging the homes when it comes to selling some of their stock and they usually get top dollar for the property sale. They also like to keep some of their houses in their growing portfolio as they have excellent positive cash flow. The plan is to have enough cash flow to cover their income. They are highly skilled in working with joint venture partner investors to acquire houses for renovation as well as in raising traditional bank finance to fund acquisitions.

The biggest thing is that they truly love their work, and I think you would have to love it. I know in the early days they sacrificed a lot, often sleeping in swags in a property whilst renovating, being away from home a lot and completely focused on their work.

The Flip Strategy Niche

This is a great strategy when you really know your market and you can negotiate getting substantial discounts on property. Of all the property niches, this one requires the investor getting the property well below market. If you get that wrong, the market is not forgiving and you can lose money. The investors that work in this niche are sometimes known as wholesalers: they acquire property and a do a quick cosmetic renovation or add value by subdividing or getting a development approval which can take time and is valuable to the next party when they on sell.

Flipping involves all the skills of the renovator niche and your most important resource is time – the investors that flip properties look to get access to the property prior to settlement so they can get in and get out quickly and have the property back on the market. Often, investors flipping property will use a lease with an option from the vendor finance niche to purchase property, to give them time to either renovate or get a development application organised. This saves having to organise traditional finance on the property

The Property Development Niche

Development is a highly specialised property niche. Whilst it can promise higher returns it has considerably more potential traps for beginners compared to the other niches. The time between paydays can be extremely long and usually the bank requires a higher capital injection. In the lending world, it is regarded as extremely high risk and finance is difficult to obtain.

A good way for a beginner to 'practice' is through renovations. This has a much shorter time frame and you also learn budgeting, dealing with builders and banks, all crucial to a development getting off the ground. Progressing through to duplexes and small developments of three to four units will help hone the skill of an aspiring property developer.

You have to know your stuff and prove it to a lender. Here is a framework to help you prepare a proposal for a lender.

- Summary of the scenario including loan amount requested.

- Location of the security: actual street address.

- Structure of the borrowing entity: trust, company individual etc.

- Have you undertaken developments in the past? If so provide details. What is the 'as is' value i.e. Land purchase price / current market value. Amount owing on the land if it is already held by you.

- Details of what are you building: no of units, is DA held? etc.

- The 'on completion' value i.e. value of the property(s) upon completion of construction.

- Will they be strata titled or held in one line?

- What is the value (or proposed value) of the fixed price building contract?

- Details of licensed builder: web site? / details of similar construction projects undertaken.

- Exit strategy: do you plan to sell or retain (are there any pre-sales in place)?

- If you plan to retain – what is estimated market rental return?

- Do you personally have any credit issues and if so, provide details.

- Any additional strengths or potential issues to know about up front?

Spending time getting this right, doing your research and having all your supporting documentation in place will not only pay huge dividends when it comes to getting funding for your development but gets you really clear on your project. In the development game time is money. You can't afford to have too much down time as it increases the holding costs, so planning is everything.

KEY POINTS

1. Having clarity around what type of niche you are in will help you avoid confusion and poor results.

2. Investing for capital growth means that the buyer is hoping that the property will over time be worth more than what it was purchased for. Capital growth largely depends on where you buy and what you buy.

3. The cash flow strategy works well on properties that tend to yield higher rental returns versus the capital used to acquire the property.

4. Vendor finance is a cash flow strategy. Vendor finance is giving someone an opportunity to own a home as opposed to renting a home. The cash flow from the property is usually more than the rental return on the same property because people are happy to pay more for a home ownership opportunity.

5. Great renovators have excellent acquisition skills; they know that they have to acquire the property below market because that is where their profit is, and that a good renovation will enhance their profit.

6. The flip strategy relies on the investor getting the property well below market. If you get that wrong, the market is not forgiving and you can lose money.

7. Property development is a highly-specialised property niche. A good way for a beginner to 'practice' is through renovations. This has a much shorter time frame and you also learn budgeting, dealing with builders and banks, all crucial to a development getting off the ground.

FELICITY'S INVESTING TIP

You have to love what you do – there is no point taking on a property niche because you can see the income potential. It doesn't matter how good the income is, if you don't love it you most likely won't stick at it.

CHAPTER 7

Finance Preparation: Getting The Finance Right

Compound interest is the eighth wonder of the world. He who understands it, earns it ... he who doesn't ... pays it.
Albert Einstein

Finance is leverage in the financial world. It is often referred to as 'gearing' where borrowed funds are used to purchase a property or some other asset. The lender will have policies as to what they feel is appropriate to lend on certain assets. The lender will value the asset or the property and lend a percentage of its value. This is known as the Loan to Valuation ratio (LVR). Getting the balance right is absolutely crucial when you are growing a property portfolio. Having your portfolio too highly geared (in other words, you have mostly all borrowed funds and very little equity) leaves you nowhere to go if something goes wrong. Conversely, not using finance to leverage means you will most likely find it extremely difficult to build a property portfolio.

Borrowing money for an investment property

The question I am most often asked is how to borrow money for an investment property. To start buying your first property requires a deposit. A good number of lenders will lend up to 95% of the property value. There is an additional cost for people who borrow over 80% of the property value, known as lender's mortgage insurance. If you are borrowing 95% of the value of the property, the mortgage insurance cost will be in the vicinity of 2.5% of the borrowed amount. Some lenders will capitalise this to the loan, which means you effectively borrow 97.5% of the value of the property. There are pros and cons here. In an upward trending market, it gets you in the property market before the property price escalates again.

You may find that paying a mortgage is similar to paying rent and justifies the mortgage insurance costs. This has rung true in recent times with interest rates being so low. Conversely, in a steady or even downward trending market you will have to work hard at paying down the loan as there is no growth to offset the cost and a bigger risk to manage the mortgage.

Borrowing at 95% of the value of the property is a great way for a first-time home buyer to enter the market. For most home buyers, buying their first home is a chance to get out of renting, and they see it as their forever home or one they plan to use to upgrade to something bigger down the track. On the other hand, the property investor's goal is to build a property portfolio to create financial freedom. Having too many properties that are too highly geared creates way more headaches than freedom. I would strongly recommend that first-time property investors save at least a 10% deposit plus the cost to complete the deal.

Not everyone would agree with me on this. One school of thought advises that you use as much of other people's money as you can when investing so that you can get into more properties, and accept mortgage insurance as just a cost of doing business. My response is to keep the end goal in mind: you want financial freedom not headaches. If you have done the work outlined in my earlier chapters and established your automatic money system, you should be on your way to saving a good cash deposit with your expenses well managed. This is about being a good steward of your money, making sure that you are constantly keeping everything in balance, including your leveraging

I have met many property investors who get in at the top of a boom with a minimal deposit, only to get caught up in the downdraft when the market corrects. All of a sudden, their property is 'upside down' and they owe more to the bank than the property is worth. The minute there is a tenancy vacancy they start to hurt because they are now funding 100% of the mortgage. If the vacancy lasts for several months, they get desperate and want to sell. When desperate they make rash decisions, and may sell well below what they paid for the property just to get rid of the headache. A lot of this can be attributed to a lack of market research, and if you combine it with an extremely high loan to valuation ratio (LVR) such as a 95% loan, you just set yourself up for failure. The difference in this same scenario for the owner-occupied home buyer is that they keep paying the mortgage for the roof over their head, and many ride out the downturn.

Home equity

The second most common question I am asked is this: How do I use the equity in my home to buy an investment property? Many of my clients have their own homes where a good amount of equity has accrued. Equity is the difference between the property value and what you owe the bank.

When you want to use your equity to buy an investment property, the most important thing to remember when instructing your mortgage broker or bank is that you want the equity portion to be a separate loan account from your home loan. This keeps your non-deductible debt separate from your deductible debt. (A chat with your accountant will help you get clarity on what is and is not tax deductible.) Often people walk into their bank and ask to open up equity from their home. The problem is that if you don't specify that you want the loan to be separate, the bank is likely to top up your existing loan and advise that you can use the redraw facility to take out the equity. Once this happens the money is 'confused', with no clear line between money for personal use and money used for investment. It then becomes an accounting nightmare to separate the non-deductable expenses from the deductible expenses.

Loan structures

A related question is about the type of structure you should instruct your bank or mortgage broker to set up. Let's look at an example.

Case Study – Mick

Mick has a property valued at $500,000 with a current mortgage of $200,000. He wants to use a further $100,000 of equity to cover the deposit and costs of purchasing another property. The

> existing $200,000 home loan should be on a principal and interest reducing loan account and the newly established $100,000 should be set up as a line of credit loan account.

A line of credit is a little like a giant credit card – it has a limit established for you to draw on and you only pay interest on the amount that you draw. The key is to get your line of credit established *before* going shopping for your investment property. It is highly recommended that you work with an experienced mortgage broker or banker when establishing the line of credit. An experienced mortgage broker or banker will also look at your future borrowing and do some mortgage planning to tailor the equity release with the proposed investment property purchases. There is no point taking out a huge line of credit against your home if it eats up all your borrowing power.

It is also worth mentioning at this point that the mortgage broker or banker should have a discussion with you about strategies to eliminate the debt on the owner-occupied portion of the loan. One thing to be aware of often when you do refinance is that the loan may be put back over a 30-year term. This has the effect of reducing your payments and can feel nice, like that first glass of wine. But it can come with a nasty hangover the next day when you realise that setting the clock back and extending the term of the loan will cost you a fortune in interest. It is fine to have the term extended but very worthwhile to maintain your existing payments. Your mortgage broker or banker can calculate what the term can be reduced to by maintaining higher payments. As previously mentioned, you can always drop down to the contractual payment if you need to.

An experienced mortgage broker or banker who gives you the right advice in the first place is worth their weight in gold. Any fee pales into insignificance over time and can save you a fortune. When you have to untangle a big mess, it is expensive, as Carol found out the hard way.

Case Study – Carol

When Carol first contacted me, she had 15 investment properties and they were 'cross collateralised'. This means the collateral from one property is also used as collateral to acquire another loan for a property. In Carol's case the collateral for all the previous properties had been used to buy the next property, so she had 15 cross collateralised properties. Carol wanted to buy more investment property but her bank said no. There was plenty of equity and Carol had good affordability. But she was stuck because, despite her loyalty, the bank decided that she had hit the ceiling regarding what they were prepared to do. Carol had purchased commercial as well as residential property. In the residential space, valuations are relatively affordable if not free with most lenders. However, valuations on a commercial property are quite expensive and can run into several thousands of dollars. As Carol had three commercial properties, the valuations cost in excess of $8,000. Unfortunately, the commercial valuations were unavoidable, however, the savings on the new loan made the exercise worth doing. Then came the challenge of completely restructuring her portfolio so that each property supported its own loan. We set Carol up with four different banks to spread her portfolio across different lenders.

At the end of the process, it was easy to see what debt related to a particular property and how much equity was in each property. If Carol now wanted to take advantage of a good deal with another lender she could, as she only needed to move one or two properties to that lender and not the whole portfolio. She also had the flexibility to go to other lenders for finance. She was not locked into one particular lender, which means that she had more control over her ability to borrow

Line of credit, offset account and redraw facilities

So what's the difference between *line of credit*, *offset account* and *redraw* facilities? Don't they all do the same thing? The answer is yes … and no. They all allow you to tap into your equity but their function and application are quite different. What you plan to do with your equity often determines which is appropriate. Adding any of these facilities to your home loan while you are growing a property portfolio can help super charge your goal to financial freedom.

As mentioned, a **line of credit** is like a giant credit card. It is set up as a separate loan to your home loan and is secured by your property. Because it is separate, bank statements on a line of credit can be provided to your accountant, who will be able to determine expenses that can be claimed on tax. A line of credit is a good way to access equity in your current property. A limit is established ready for you to draw on and it is useful to do this prior to going shopping for investment property. The idea is to use the line of credit to pay for the deposit and cost of the new purchase of an investment property and raise a loan (say 80% of the valuation) on the new investment property purchase.

An **offset account** is an everyday transactional account that is linked to your home loan. Whatever funds are held in the offset account are used to offset interest on your home loan. An offset account is one the most powerful ways to save tens of thousands of dollars on your home. Used in conjunction with a debt elimination strategy, you can repay your home loan in an extraordinarily short period of time. Imagine that you had $50,000 in your offset account and you had a $400,000 home loan. Interest would only be charged $350,000 instead of $400,000. The $50,000 is easily accessible should you need to use it at any time. The interest on your home loan that is offset by the funds in your offset account is tax free.

A **redraw** facility means that the extra payments you have made on your home are available for withdrawal at any time. Often lenders will 'top up' your home loan so that you can access your equity, the funds are then available in your redraw account. Exercise caution if you are offered a topup on your home loan to access your equity and you are planning to use the funds to invest in an investment property as this is the wrong structure. The correct way to access your equity is to have a separate loan established. The equity released needs to be kept separate from your home loan to keep your non-deductible expenses getting mixed up with your deductible expenses.

Access to finance for self-employed people

One of the biggest headaches for a self-employed person is qualifying for finance. It is more difficult for a business owner to complete the foundational steps towards financial freedom compared to someone with a wage or salary. A business owner needs to apply the foundational steps to both their home finances and their business finances, as well as do a lot of strategic planning in order for the business to grow.

When you are looking for finance, the bank will want to verify your income through the business financials and tax returns. A major task for an accountant is to minimise a business owner's tax liability. They look for as many business expenses as possible to reduce their income in order for the business owner's tax liability to be reduced. This is where a conflict often arises for the business owner: they report low income to the tax department but when it comes time to borrow, this is the only income figure that the bank accepts.

The business owner can often see an upward trend in figures when approaching the bank for finance and knows that the figures won't appear in the returns until after the cut-off date the following financial year. In this situation, many banks use a 'lo doc' (or 'lite doc') loan, however this is not without its downside. A lo doc loan is generally more expensive in interest rate and fees. Income still has to be verified either through BAS statements, bank statements or an accountant's letter. Lo doc lending can solve the problem of getting into a loan in the short term but you definitely need an exit strategy enabling you to move into a more affordable loan down the track. The exit strategy is the production of the financials and tax returns in the one to two years after your lo doc loan is established.

My advice is that if you want to use the traditional banks to borrow to grow either your business or a property portfolio, pay yourself a wage that reflects what you are really worth.

If you had to employ someone in your business to do what you do, how much would you pay them? The problem for many business owners, particularly small business owners, is that they don't pay themselves. We have a dreadful phobia this country about paying tax, to the point where people will do just about anything not to. (Negative gearing is a classic example of this and I discuss it in Chapter 6)

Finally, if you own a business, you would be wise to have a conversation with your accountant about your goals for your business. All too often, business owners dump their receipts with the accountant who duly prepares a tax return. Whist preparing tax returns may appear to be their primary function, many accountants have the ability to provide valuable advice on business growth. A conversation with your accountant around your short, medium and long-term business objectives could be extremely important in helping you achieve financial freedom.

KEY POINTS

1. Finance is leverage in the financial world. Understanding leverage is a great asset for a property investor with a growing portfolio.

2. Some property investors get in at the top of the boom with a minimal deposit only to get caught up in the downdraft when the market corrects.

3. Being a good steward of your money means making sure that you are constantly keeping everything in balance. This includes your leveraging.

4. Have your finance organised before you go shopping for your investment property.

5. The experienced mortgage broker or banker will look at your future borrowing and do some mortgage planning to tailor the equity release with the proposed investment property purchases.

6. Instruct your mortgage broker or bank that you want the equity portion that you are opening up to be in a separate loan account from your home loan. This will keep your non-deductible debt separate from your deductible debt.

7. A line of credit is like a giant credit card. It is set up as a separate loan to your home loan and is secured by your property.

8. An offset account is an everyday transactional account that is linked to your home loan. Whatever funds are held in the offset account are used to offset interest on your home loan.

9. A redraw facility means that the extra payments that you have made on your home are available at any time.

10. An experienced mortgage broker or banker who gives you the right advice is worth their weight in gold.

11. If you think paying for expert advice is expensive, try ignorance.

12. If you are a small business owner and want to borrow, make sure you pay yourself a wage.

13. Remember that if you are paying tax you are making money.

FELICITY'S INVESTING TIP

If you are starting out on your journey as a property investor, get your financial foundation set up and understand how leverage or gearing can exponentially increase your returns.

SECTION 2 : ACQUISITION

Chapter 8

How To Research The Market

Research is creating new knowledge.
Neil Armstrong

Market research is a valuable skill when it comes to investing in property. Not only can you work out the price that a property is worth but you can start to see trends in the property market.

Rules for investing in property

I was fortunate to learn about personal rules for investing from my good friend and mentor, John Burley, and I have adopted many of his personal rules as my own. Having a set of rules helps you develop a laser focus on the type of property you want acquire and how much you want to pay for it. It helps you sort the wheat from the chaff very quickly and acquire properties that fit your criteria. The logical thing about rules is that if you break them, you have to wear the consequences. Having rules keeps you from making too many mistakes.

The rules that have served me well are these:

1. **Operate with integrity**. Reputation is huge. When people can trust you and know that you deliver what you promise, business will naturally come your way.

2. **My rules and my rules only**. Playing the game with someone else's rules doesn't work. One of my rules is to buy property that has positive cash flow. So to buy something with negative cash flow, then hope and pray that it will eventually turn into positive cash flow is a deal I would never consider.

3. **Know my market, niche and return on investment**. The clearer that I am on my market, game (niche) and return, the faster I can acquire the exact deal that will produce the results that I am looking for.

4. **Buy wholesale**. This one is a biggie. There's no point buying a property for retail, it doesn't matter how nice it is! Let's face it, I am never going to live in it. As investor, I need to be focused on what discount I can I buy it for.

5. **Profit at purchase**. The profit in a property happens at purchase, and this links to the previous rule: buy wholesale, not retail.

6. **Buy when the numbers make sense**. Never buy with emotions. The property is a commodity, to be acquired for the sole purpose of making money and not because it is a pretty house that will look good in your portfolio.

7. **Invest for the long term**. My own property portfolio reminds me at times of cricket: there are rules and it takes a while. For the most part, a cricket match is won by hitting ones and twos with a six every so often. If you try to hit too many sixes, you generally lose. Property investing is very similar. It takes time and requires consistent effort (the ones and twos), and every once in a while, an amazing deal comes across your desk (a six).

   I have seen people attracted to property investing because they think they can make a fortune overnight. These people often have poor financial foundations and are looking to hit a six on their first deal that will solve all their money woes. Unfortunately, it doesn't work that way and if you expect it to, you will often just exacerbate an already dysfunctional financial position. I have seen this happen in the vendor finance industry. People saw it as a way of creating quick capital gains in a 12-month period. In fact, vendor finance was always meant to be a long-term cash flow strategy, not a quick flip for the capital gain.

8. **Ride the winners and cut the losers**. Once in a while you end up with a 'dog' in your portfolio and by that, I mean it just doesn't perform. If it is not performing and is losing you money, cut it loose. If you keep it in the hope that it will recover, you find that all the time and energy you devote to this property will keep you from other opportunities.

9. **Continuing education**. Just when you think you know everything you discover how little you actually do know. The world is a changing place and keeping up can be a challenge. I remember how the first seminar I went to was so useful it blew my mind. These days I go to workshops and seminars to get that little gold nugget of information, something that will help me improve what I do. My library at home just keeps growing and it never ceases to amaze me just how much there is to learn.

10. **Surround yourself with a professional team and pay them well**. This one is also huge for me. I don't know where I would be without my lawyer, accountant, mentors and many others that have contributed to my success. Their advice and support is priceless.

Tools for market research

There are many programs that can help you analyse the market, such a RP Data (corelogic.com.au) and Real Estate Investar (realestateinvestar.com.au) and Residex (residex.com.au) to name a few. Even realestate.com.au and domain.com.au have research tools available to help you make decisions about what you are prepared to pay for a property. They are also good if you are tracking a particular property to see if there are price reductions or tracking what the median house price is in a particular suburb.

As mentioned, the *median* house price is the midway point of all the houses sold over a set period (monthly, yearly, quarterly, etc.). That is, if there were 101 houses sold during the month, the median house price would be the house price in the middle i.e., that has 50 house prices above it and 50 house prices below it. The median differs to the *mean* price, which equates to the average price and calculated by adding the sold prices together and dividing the result by the number of sales. The main reason the median price is used rather than the mean is because it is a more accurate indicator of the market, as it reflects the sample size being used. That said, if you have a larger number of more expensive (or cheaper) houses in the sample, it can skew the median house price and may not be as accurate.

You could take a market analyst approach and research everything online. However, in my experience, the most effective method is to visit the area you are interested in. Burn some shoe leather whilst walking around talking to local real estate agents and the neighbours of houses that you may be looking to purchase. Here is what a young investor wrote to me about a property he was thinking of purchasing:

> *I am looking to purchase a property in an area where all the other properties are listed at offers over $325,000. The property is 3-bed, 1-bath, 1-car in perfectly fine condition. The problem is there are power lines running over the rear of the property and this is the reason no one else is interested because it is listed well under what other properties have been selling for. A very similar property in the same street sold 2 months ago for $365,000.*

Regardless of the statistical data, when you go to apply for traditional finance the bank will send the valuer out to value the individual property. The fact is that if a property is impacted by power lines, most people will view this as a health risk that they are not prepared to take. The majority of people may have trouble funding such a property due to adverse remarks that the valuer may add to the valuation report to the bank. Such a property is not likely to be a good buy and the price is not a genuine discount even though it is $40,000 under what the other houses are in the area. A genuine discount would be when a property is really worth $365,000 and someone is prepared to sell at $325,000 because they want a quick sale.

Events such as murder or suicide on a property will also dramatically affect the sale and hence the value. Once a bank valuer makes an adverse comment on why a property is at a reduced sale price, it will alert the banks to the risk and this will impact on your ability to borrow, especially if the borrowings are in mortgage insurance territory.

And now for the million-dollar question: how much do you pay for a property? A property is really only worth what someone is prepared to pay for it. Statistical analysis will help you with comparisons, as mentioned. Other things that impact on your offer include how long the property has been on the market; where it 'fits' compared with similar properties; whether the vendor has previously dropped the price; and the property's condition. Bear in mind that if you purchase a property that needs repairs this will impact your ability to borrow for that property. The bank may request to see that you have funds available to do repairs or decline the loan because it is not a good security risk for them.

Case Study – Georgia

One of my investor clients Georgia wanted to buy a townhouse at Tweed Heads NSW. As an estimator for a construction company, Georgia was very skilled at costing out renovations. The townhouse that she wanted to buy had termites. The vendor had removed the wall in the bedroom to show the damage. Most people shied away from the property as termites can mean expensive repairs. Georgia knew that it would cost her less than $10,000 to treat and repair the termite damage. She was able to negotiate a $90,000 discount. The problem was that although the bank was happy to lend her the money, they didn't want the property as security for the loan because of the termite damage.

Georgia approached the vendor to ask if she could access the property to do the work as soon as they had exchanged contracts. The vendor agreed and within a week and half the termites were treated and the damage repaired. Georgia also managed to paint the inside of the property. The bank's valuer was then asked to inspect the property after the repairs were done and the bank was happy to lend the money and take the property as security for the loan.

Where to invest

Deciding where to invest after you have done all the research often will come down to how accessible the area is to you. I personally like areas that are in close proximity to where I live, however I did buy many houses that were up to four hours' drive away. Let's face it, if there is ever a major problem, even if you have a property manager, it is you that has to fix it once everyone else has run for the hills. Many investors like to invest interstate and globally. In my opinion, however, the further the property is away from you, the stronger the management has to be and the more prepared you have to be to jump in your car or on a plane to fix a problem.

Case Study – Damage to Property

One of my properties in Tamworth NSW, a four-hour drive west of my place, was once badly trashed. Whilst the property manager was happy to organise the police report, I still needed to jump in the car and drive to get a good sense of how bad the damage was and to make sure we got the correct information to the insurance company. On my drive, I moaned about how inconvenient it was to have to drop everything and I was grateful that it wasn't any further. On the other hand, it did give me an opportunity to check up on my other houses in the area and meet with the local agents.

When I finally arrived at the property I noticed some local kids sitting on the roof flicking off the roof tiles. I had this sinking feeling that it wasn't going to be easy to prevent more damage and an even worse feeling of stopping further damage to the repaired work. I spoke to a local builder and he suggested erecting temporary fencing with barbed wire along the top and a big skull-and-crossbones sign with the words WARNING ASBESTOS. It did the trick and we got the house repaired. In fact, it looked brand new inside and we were able to raise the rent and find a tenant quickly. To this day, the house continues to provide positive cash flow.

KEY POINTS

1. Having a set of property investment rules will help you develop a laser focus on the type of property you want to acquire and how much you want to pay for it. It helps you sort the wheat from the chaff very quickly and acquire properties that fit your criteria.

2. Helpful tools include RP Data (corelogic.com.au) and Real Estate Investar (realestateinvestar.com.au) and Residex (residex.com.au). Even realestate.com.au and domain.com.au have research tools available to help you make decisions about what you are prepared to pay for a property.

3. Market research tools are great up to a point, however nothing beats actually physically viewing the property, the area and talking to people.

4. If a major problem occurs with your property, nobody will want to know about it. Just know that the buck stops with you, so be prepared to drop everything.

FELICITY'S INVESTING TIP

Knowledge is power. If you are armed with good statistical research along with your own personal enquiries, the effort will pay off and more importantly, it will give you the confidence to submit an offer.

CHAPTER 9

The Numbers Don't Lie

The fact is that one of the earliest lessons I learned in business was that balance sheets and income statements are fiction, cash flow is reality.
Chris Chocola

Buying an investment property is not about guessing whether or not it will make you money. Being clear on your niche and how much you expect the property to make will ensure that it meets the objective of making money.

If your only objective is to reduce your tax, you will lose money. Many people are sold on the idea of saving tax when they buy an investment property. In order to save on tax, you have to *lose* money on your property investment. This strategy is known as negative gearing. The ATO allows you write off any of the losses you have on your investment property against your personal income. Sounds good, but what's the reality? As an example, let's say you are earning $100,000 gross annually and your tax rate is 35 cents in the dollar. Your tax bill for the year will be $35,000. Let's also say your investment property loses $10,000 in the financial year. The $10,000 loss is deducted from your gross income of $100,000, making it $90,000. Your tax is then calculated on $90,000, making the tax bill $31,500 instead of $35,000. You might have met the objective of 'reducing your tax' by $3,500. But it has cost you $6,500 to do so. The crazy part is that the property cost you money, and that money came out of your pocket! Some people argue that the capital growth of the property will exceed the losses. Sometimes it does and sometimes it doesn't and at the end of the day, this is a hope and pray strategy.

If your objective is to make money, you need to look at a property from its income earning potential versus the capital outlay involved. You can very easily do a 'back of the envelope' calculation that requires finding out what the weekly rent potential is versus the value of the property. If you want to achieve a 5% return you would look for a property where the rent is the same as the first three digits in the purchase price. For example, a $400,000 house that rents for $400 per week gives roughly a 5% return. In fact: ($400 X 52 ÷ $400,000) = 5.2%. Try it – it works! Given that interest rates are at an all-time low, it becomes easier to seek a neutral or positive cash flow on the property.

Vendor finance is a cash flow strategy and a great way to get excellent cash flow from a property. People are willing to pay more than rent for the opportunity to own. Many vendor finance properties will make $600 - $800 per month, clear of all expenses, including interest, rates and insurance. Whilst one house making $600 - $800 per month doesn't appear to be too significant, 10 houses making $600 - $800 per month becomes $6000 - $8000 per month and that *is* significant.

There are a lot of costs in the actual buying of a property, including stamp duty, legal fees and finance costs. Often these costs can be in excess of 5% of the property's purchase price. For example, the costs to purchase a $400,000 house can be in the vicinity of $20,000. If you then sell that same property, you also have selling costs and it wouldn't be unreasonable to expect them to be in the vicinity of $10,000. This is where many renovators and people who flip property get caught: before they can even begin to make a profit there is $30,000 worth of buying and selling costs to account for. This is where the skill of knowing what the numbers are comes in, so that you can negotiate the property to a price that can cope with the expenses. There is no point buying a property at full price and expecting to renovate in order to make money. At best, you may cover your renovation costs but it is unlikely you will cover your buying and selling costs. Therefore, you will lose money.

When holding a property, it is also important to know what the ongoing costs are. Running a property is like running a business where keeping expenses under control is paramount. The main expenses are your interest cost, repairs and maintenance, property management, rates and insurance. Interest will more than likely be the biggest cost. Whilst most repairs and maintenance are necessary, it is always worthwhile getting a good understanding of *why* a repair needs to be done in the first place. Some tenants have a habit of passing on a repair to the landlord when the damage was actually caused by them. Often the property manager just goes ahead and gets things repaired because they are urgent. However, it is worth digging a little deeper to find the underlying cause as sometimes it is not a repair for wear and tear but for damage caused by the tenant.

In one of my rental properties, I was receiving a recurring plumbing bill. When we were asked to get the plumber out again shortly after the first request, I asked the property manager to speak to the plumber and ask for a report on why the plumbing was blocked again. It turned out the tenants' children were putting toys down the toilet, causing it to block. The tenant was advised that they were to pay for the plumbing themselves. It is one thing to pay for normal wear and tear on a property, and another matter entirely to pay for damage by a tenant. This experience alerted me to make sure that the property manager always got reports on what had caused the reported damage. A good property manager is worth their weight in gold. I am always happy to pay good money for an effective property manager and I never haggle over fees. In the end, I save way more money than I spend when I have quality management.

There are many property investment programs on the market to help you analyse, collate and maintain data on your investment property. One of the great things about property is that once you have the finance, tenant or occupant and manager all in place, you can set and forget for a period, reviewing each property on an annual basis to assess its performance and tweak if necessary to keep things running like a well-oiled machine. Annual reviews on your portfolio are important to show how you have grown over a 12-month period and what is possible going forward.

Deciding on what you are prepared to pay for a property comes down to your niche and your plan for the property. In the following chapter, I cover strategies on working with agents and negotiating. It will all come down to your personal rules. For example, when I first started, I only wanted to buy properties with positive cash flow within a one-hour drive of my home. That was a personal rule of mine.

KEY POINTS

1. Buying an investment property is not about guessing whether or not it will make you money.

2. If your only objective is to reduce your tax, you will lose money.

3. You can very easily do a 'back of the envelope' calculation that requires finding out what the weekly rent potential is versus the value of the property. If you want to achieve a 5% return you would look for a property where the rent is the same as the first three digits in the purchase price. For example, a $400,000 house that rents for $400 per week gives roughly a 5% return ($400 X 52 ÷ $400,000) = 5.2%.

4. When holding a property, it is also important to know the ongoing costs.

5. Deciding on what you are prepared to pay for a property comes down to your niche and your plan for the property.

FELICITY'S INVESTING TIP

Never make a purchase decision based solely on the potential capital appreciation or tax benefits. A purchase decision should be made on the property's ability to produce cash flow. Cash flow is like ice cream in a bowl. The ice cream is better if you add whipped cream (capital appreciation) and a cherry (tax benefit). The whipped cream and cherry make it really nice and are great bonuses if you can get them.

Chapter 10

Deal or No Deal

A negotiator should observe everything. You must be part Sherlock Holmes, part Sigmund Freud.

Victor Kiam

I did a lot of hands-on property investment training in the US and one of the exercises that I am most grateful for taught me to submit lots of written offers. The object was to find a property that suited the numbers that you had researched. The exercise involved connecting with an agent and communicating to them that you were an investor looking to purchase an investment property if (and only if) the numbers suited your criteria. This probably sounds simple enough, but when your emotions get in the way the exercise can become really difficult.

All of a sudden you feel intimated by the process and afraid of being told No. It gets worse when the agent tells you that your offer is insulting to the vendor and wants to call you every name under the sun. The reality is, you need to be a very clear communicator: clear on your research, clear on your intention and very clear on what you are prepared to pay for a property. Once the agent understands what you want to achieve, you can then start the process of writing lots of offers. I found this process a valuable way to develop the emotional muscle required to find the deal that you want. Writing lots of offers really is the only way to become skilled at acquiring good deals. It requires you to find a reliable agent, someone who understands that you buy according to the numbers and not according to how you feel. The key here is to find the agent first, then the deal.

Working with real estate agents

Learning to work with agents has been absolutely central to my success as a property investor. Spending time developing a strong relationship with agents allows me much broader scope when submitting offers. Often, agents bring me deals to consider as well.

If you don't find the time to develop a relationship with an agent and you fire off offers, things can sometimes get a little intense. If a low offer comes in from an investor where there is very little relationship with the agent, the delivery of the offer can suffer. The agent has very little information about the investor other than that they are obviously firing off offers in the hope that if they throw enough mud at the wall something will stick. They are obliged by law to submit the offer regardless of how low it is, or whether or not they think the vendor will accept it. You can imagine the scenario: the agent receives an offer out of the blue. It is likely to be submitted to the vendor with a sarcastic tone and anything but enthusiasm. The response back to investor can range from a simple No to an extremely rude No complete with expletives! It's true that I have seen investors work this way and occasionally pick up good deals that even surprise the agent. I prefer to build long-term business relationships with people and this has served me very well as I have been able to acquire many great deals.

The agent needs to understand that you are a property investor who is cashed up and ready to buy, looking for a deal that is significantly below the asking price. Once the agent is clear on your objective, the communication of your offer is made with gusto and a lot less angst.

Case Study – Jeannie

Jeannie is an investor friend who scans the national market looking for properties that have been on the market for more than six months. As a cash buyer who doesn't use traditional bank finance in her transactions, Jeannie can be very flexible in where she buys as it doesn't involve a bank deciding whether or not they will lend in a particular area. Jeannie looks at the trend for when the properties were first listed and she watches as prices are reduced. Sometimes these properties sit on the market for more than twelve months in areas with no capital growth whatsoever, but they often rent like crazy. When a property has dropped more than 50% of its original value, Jeannie contacts the agent and makes an offer. She doesn't put too much time into building a relationship with the agent but instead spends her time and energy on research. More often than not, an agent is thrilled to hear from an investor like Jeannie.

The agents I work with often have me on their books and contact me as investment opportunities arise. If I am seriously considering buying a property, I also go for a walk and see what I can find out from neighbours. It is often surprising what neighbours know and what an agent does not know. This can help when it comes to negotiating the deal.

Negotiating – the price is right

Most people think negotiating is about either winning or losing. In other words, they are focused on their preferred outcome and not on what the other party wants. The reality is that you really can't get what you want unless the other person gets what they want too. If they don't actually tell you what they want, it is up to you to ask lots of questions and listen hard to extract the information you need.

It is at this point that the rubber meets the road and all your work up to now comes together. You have done the market research, you have developed relationships with agents and you are now ready to submit offers.

When I first started in vendor finance, I chose to work within an hour's drive of my home. The kids were little and I needed to make sure that I was in close proximity, so this was my main criterion as I looked for properties. I started working in an area south of Newcastle, in a suburb called Gateshead. The area was mainly ex-housing commission houses, all with three bedrooms and one bathroom and some with a garage. In fact, the floor plan in every single house was the same, with variations including mirror reversing. I remember that these homes looked like the one that my grandparents owned in Serpentine Crescent, north Balgowlah, Sydney. Today these Balgowlah homes sell for well in excess of $1.5 million.

Over time Gateshead has become mostly owner-occupied and was just starting to become appealing for being just five minutes from the major shopping hub, Charlestown Square. It still had the stigma of being a housing commission area, which had kept the prices low. The properties made ideal homes for people who wanted a home ownership opportunity, as they were affordable and in an area that had great services.

I met many of the local agents and told them what I was looking for. I was very specific about the price range and that fact that I wasn't concerned if the house was a little tired and needed some basic cosmetic work. I would drive around the suburb on a daily basis looking at how the properties were kept. You would be surprised at how many had overgrown gardens and lawns, to the point that the For Sale sign could be almost completely hidden. This was always a strong indication that the people just needed to get rid of the property. Sometimes it was a tenant who hadn't bothered taking care of the property once they knew that the landlord was selling. Sometimes it was a divorce situation where the female was still living in the house with the kids and the male had left. The state of the property told the story, and the story was that these vendors needed to get out and were, for the most part, highly negotiable.

I loved the properties that had a couple of holes in the wall. This always looked way worse than it really was. I think that when you walk into these properties they look angry and this turns so many people off. The reality is that it takes a handy man very little time to patch a hole and put some paint over the top. These properties look great when the lawn is mowed. I would also get a cleaner in to sugar soap the walls, scrub the kitchen and bathroom, vacuum the carpets and dust every nook and cranny. In fact, the lady I employed also used to clean my own house and she loved getting the extra work. She later created a business out of detailing houses for real estate agents.

The properties that had the most potential were the ones that smelt really bad. Many of my property investor friends refer to this as 'the smell of money'. This sort of property required more than just a clean and a few minor repairs. It required the carpet to be ripped up and as most of the houses had floor boards, it was often more affordable to sand and polish them rather than replace the carpet. Also, the polyurethane got rid of the cat pee smell entirely! These houses would then present beautifully and it was easy to rent them or on-sell them with a greater margin on vendor finance.

The research that I did made the negotiations seem relatively easy. The fact was, I could identify the properties that were likely to be highly negotiable. Often I would talk to the agent and ask how come the property looked so untidy. This was always a great opening question, and the responses were amazing. I would hear that the tenant had been nothing but a pain and the landlord was so over dealing with them that they just wanted the property sold. Another common response was that the owners had had a nasty separation and were desperate to move on. Sometimes the situation was that the owners had purchased elsewhere and really needed to sell so they could focus on their new property.

Most of the agents that I worked with were really helpful and excited to get an offer on the properties in this category. It wasn't hard to get a 15% - 20% discount because the vendors needed a quick sale. This goes back to what I said earlier about negotiation: in order to get what I want, I had to make sure that the other people got what they want. In these situations, the vendors wanted a quick sale and as an investor I wanted a good deal. It was win-win.

My offers were always written as this allowed me to keep track of them and also demonstrated that I was serious. The written offers also allowed me to negotiate on terms. For example, it was really important to me to have access to the property before it settled so I could do the necessary maintenance or repairs so that I would not have too much downtime once I owned the property. The other reason was it gave me time to market the property appropriately to find the right occupant. The biggest cost when holding a property is the interest bill on the loan. Time is money so anything that could be done prior to settlement date should be done to alleviate the holding costs.

Buying property with little or no deposit

The key to buying property with little or no deposit is to make lots of offers asking the vendor if they will accept terms such as 80% of the money now and 20% over time. In this case the terms of how the property is acquired becomes more important than the actual price that the property is acquired for. The case study below details how Connor acquired a property without using any of his own money.

Case Study – Connor

Connor is aged 23 and he wanted to start buying investment property now, however the problem was that even though he was saving it seemed like it would take him forever to get into the market. Just when he had saved enough deposit the market had moved and he was required to save more. Connor had done all the right things with regards to establishing his financial foundation first. He was working full time and was also studying commerce and economics at university, he lived at home and didn't have many expenses and saved most of his income. Frustrated with the length of time it was taking he decided to be creative and acquire a property where by the vendor would accept some of the money now for the property and some money later. Connor started building relationships with real estate agents and let them know that he was keen to acquire a property with these terms. Connor made twenty-three offers before one was accepted. Not everyone will accept an offer with terms, therefore the high rejection rate on the offers. The important thing to remember is to keep going and making offers and not give up because someone says no.

The reason that Connor's twenty third offer was accepted was that the terms suited the vendor. In this case the vendor did not need all the money today and was happy to receive a return on his money that was higher than bank interest. The vendor was also happy that he did not have to reduce the price of the property to sell it. The negotiation was perfect because it was win/win for everyone.

Connors deal looked like this.

Purchase Price $500,000
Closing costs $ 25,000
Total $525,000

Connor approached my mortgage company to assist him with obtaining a suitable loan. The bank agreed to lend him 80% of the value the property. See the first mortgage details below;

Loan amount: $400,000

Interest: 3.99%

Term: 30 years (Principal and Interest)

Monthly Repayment: 1907.36

The vendor agreed to "carry back" a loan of $125,000. This amount covered Connor's deposit of $100,000 and the costs of $25,000 he needed to completed the deal. Details of the vendor's loan;

Loan Amount: 125,000

Interest: 4.19%

Term: 3 years (Interest Only)

Monthly Payment: $436.46

When the property settles, the vendor will receive $375,000 and the other $125,000 will be repaid to vendor in 3 years' time. Connor plans to pay down the vendor loan faster than the agreed terms above and will refinance the property in 3 years' time to pay out the balance of the vendor's loan.

Connor was able to borrow 105% of the property's value and not use any of his own money.

KEY POINTS

1. You need to be a very clear communicator: clear on your research, clear on your intention and very clear on what you are prepared to pay for a property.

2. Writing lots of offers really is the only way to become skilled at acquiring good deals. This requires you to find a good agent who understands you are an investor who buys property according to the numbers and not on how you feel about the property.

3. Learning to work with agents is paramount for a successful property investor.

4. Most people think negotiating is about either winning or losing. In other words, they are focused on their preferred outcome and not on what the other party wants. The reality is that you really can't get what you want unless the other person gets what they want.

5. The properties with the most potential are the ones that smell really bad. Many property investors refer to this as 'the smell of money'.

6. Being highly organised with finance, being able to communicate clearly what you want and understanding what the vendor wants all make for successful negotiation.

FELICITY'S INVESTING TIP

Never buy a property based on emotion, but always based on the numbers. Let's face it, you are never going to live there.

SECTION 3 :

POSSESSION

CHAPTER 11

Taking Possession

An investment in knowledge pays the best interest.
Benjamin Franklin

Taking Possession before Settlement

Following your market research and successful price negotiation, the property is now finally available to you. If you were also successful in negotiating terms that allowed you possession before settlement, you have the welcome opportunity to prepare the property according to your niche. The investor looking to improve their positive cash flow position may want to do a cosmetic renovation to increase the current rent. The investor looking to sell the property on vendor finance may organise marketing for a suitable occupant. The renovator can save on holding costs during the possession to settlement period.

Possession enables you to legally enter the premises, subject to the terms and conditions of the agreed sale contract. Possession is not ownership, which occurs on the day of settlement. For that reason alone, you should make sure that the property is insured as soon as you exchange the contract and definitely prior to taking possession. It is better to double up on insurance rather than rely on the seller's insurance or risk the worst case scenario where no one takes responsibility for insurance.

I would highly recommend having a chat with your lawyer about the terms that you want in the contract, such as early possession or completing renovations. These terms should be communicated in your offer as discussed in Chapter 10.

Taking Possession after Settlement

Even if you have not been able to negotiate possession prior to settlement, the good news is that you are now the legal owner. The same thing applies to insurance; it is always better to insure the property from the time you exchange contracts on the property as opposed to settlement. You don't want the hassle of relying on the seller's insurance.

A *condition report* summarises your observations of the property at the time that you hand over the keys to the tenant or occupant. I highly recommended that photos are taken to support the report. If there is a dispute and you need the tenant to take responsibility for damage, the report will prove the condition of the property at the time of hand over.

A condition report is especially required if the property is being rented and you have collected a bond. A condition report should also be completed for properties that are under a rent-to-buy agreement as they are subject to the same rules as standard rentals. If the property is under an instalment contract a condition report is not necessary, however it is wise to have one as it helps in times of claiming on insurance if the occupant has caused damage.

Qualifying your tenant or potential purchaser for your property is critical to the success of building a large portfolio. Just as a bad occupant will cost you money, a good one will make you money. In most cases, people rely on a property manager to qualify a tenant for a rental property. This works quite well as property managers have access to tenancy blacklist databases. Privately owned, these contain the details of people who have breached their rental contract. The databases are used by agents to screen prospective tenants to make sure they are reliable and likely to be respectful of a rental property. If a tenant has breached their rental agreement, or done something deemed wrong in regards to your rental property and agreement, they are listed in the database.

I had a rental tenant abscond while owing me over $1200 in rent for a property in Tamworth. Several years down the track I got a call from an agent in Byron Bay saying that my ex-tenants wanted to make good the rent so they could be removed from the database.

Possession Issues relating to Vendor Finance

It was satisfying to get my money back and the experience made me very cautious when dealing with people who want to come through my vendor finance program. Whilst I did have access to the tenancy database I made it one of my policies for the applicant to provide me with their rental log. This didn't tell me how they would look after my house, so I always met them and looked at how they kept their car. If it was full of discarded fast-food wrappers, I figured that if they didn't take pride in their own car how was my house going to look after one year? Sometimes it is very tempting to drop your qualification standards when your property has been vacant, but in the long run it never serves you well. You are better off with a longer vacancy time than a second-rate occupant.

The next most obvious enquiry to make is whether the applicants can afford the rent or the vendor finance repayment. Their source(s) of income need to be verified. A number of factors come into play, such as the number of people that the income or incomes are supporting and what other expenses they have. At the end of the day, you need a well-designed application form that asks for details about assets, liabilities, income and commitments. For a vendor finance applicant, enquiries should be made about their living expenses and also an exit strategy for how they are going to move from vendor finance to bank finance in case you don't want them to remain in the vendor finance contract. The point here is not to expect to move someone on in a short period of time. Remember that vendor finance is a long-term cash flow strategy not a quick flip strategy.

I have found that it can be difficult for vendor finance clients to negotiate bank finance so that they can complete their purchase. Not all banks will acknowledge a vendor finance contract. Obstacles may include:

- Vendor finance payments may not be considered 'genuine savings'
- A number of banks only accept the 'contract price' on a loan application and not the actual valuation
- Trying to explain to a bank what vendor finance is
- The following four points can guide you.

At times it has been an uphill battle, but I have found lenders that are open to the idea. In fact, many of them like the fact that a client is 'road tested' and that I can produce an excellent repayment history. Often the vendor finance payment is higher than the loan repayment and this gives a lender reassurance about the client's affordability.

So how do you know when it is time for your client to move from vendor finance to bank finance?

Equity

Does your client have at least 10%, or even better 20%, equity in the property? Bear in mind that the property will be valued by a bank valuer, so the equity will be determined by what the bank thinks the property is worth and not what it says on your contract. Hopefully, the property value will have gone up since you commenced the contract. Your client has three ways of creating equity:

- Paying down the contract
- Doing renovations
- Benefiting from natural appreciation in property prices

Continuous employment

Does your client have two years of continuous employment (a change in employment is OK as long as it is in the same industry)? The situation that is really problematic is changing from working for a boss to being self-employed. A self-employed person needs to have at least two years trading in their own business before they can apply for a loan.

Income

Does your client have the income to meet the loan payments? The best indicator of this is that they have a good track record with you, the vendor financier. A mortgage broker or bank will do an affordability check to confirm that your client can afford the loan.

Clean credit

Does your client have clean credit? A very small default such as a telephone bill default of a $150 can prevent your client from qualifying for bank finance. Clients that have suffered bankruptcy will also find it difficult to qualify for a loan as generally speaking, a 20% equity position will be required.

The most successful vendor finance transactions that move to bank finance are the ones that have been in a vendor finance contract for around five years; where the occupant has 10% – 20% equity in the property, a good repayment history, stable employment and clean credit. A mortgage broker experienced in vendor finance can assist with the whole process.

What does your client do if they can't meet one of the four criteria above? The best thing for them to do is make an appointment with a mortgage broker who is experienced in vendor finance and can work out a strategy on how to get a loan. They may be surprised at how close they are to qualifying.

KEY POINTS

1. Possession is not ownership; ownership occurs on the day of settlement. For that reason alone, you should make sure that the property is insured as soon as you exchange the contract.

2. Taking possession prior to settlement can allow you to organise an occupant and help keep the holding costs at bay.

3. Qualifying your tenant or potential purchaser for your property is critical to the success of building a large portfolio. A bad occupant will cost you money, while a good occupant will make you money.

FELICITY'S INVESTING TIP

Be creative and consider negotiating terms as well as price. Depending on your niche, it can be valuable to negotiate possession before settlement.

CHAPTER 12

Profit From The Small Things

It is not the beauty of a building you should look at; it is the construction of the foundation that will stand the test of time.

David Allan Coe

A cosmetic makeover doesn't have to cost a lot to dramatically improve the cash flow on your property. Start with the property's façade: does it have street appeal? Surprisingly little things like a garden makeover can lift a property from drab to wow for a few hundred dollars. Replacing or painting the front door can also significantly increase street appeal.

Case Study – Garden makeover

One of my homes in the Hunter Valley had begun to look really tired. The front fence was rickety and the garden neglected. When the property became vacant, I hired a garden handyman to weed and pull out plants that didn't suit. He replaced them with plants that made sense for the front garden and rejuvenated the existing lawn. I hired fencing people to replace the rickety fence with a new picket fence. For the cost of $2,500 it increased my rent by $30 per week. The payback period on my investment was a little over 1.5 years.

A *payback period* is the length of time required for an investment to recover its initial outlay in terms of profit or savings. As in my Hunter Valley case, if the makeover costs $2500 and you get an increase in rent of $30 per week, the payback period is 18 months. Anything after that is pure profit. And yes, I could have done the job for less if I had done it myself, however I believe that I can make more money by doing what I do best and leaving other tasks for people who are much better at them than I am.

As you walk through the house, have a look at what you can do that doesn't cost too much yet can have a dramatic impact on your rental return. Often just giving the interior a fresh coat of paint makes a house look really fresh and inviting. Replacing the doors on existing kitchen cabinets helps modernise a kitchen. Look at the doors, door handles, tap fittings, paint colours and interior floor coverings and pay attention to the details that may pay dividends in rental return. Bathrooms and kitchens are great places for small cosmetic makeovers, because you can consider upgrading tap fittings, benchtops and splashbacks for a reasonable cost. Even replacing old appliances can be a relatively affordable investment that will bring you a good bang for your buck.

Look at fixtures and fittings too. One of my houses recently required some electrical work so whilst the electrician was there I asked him to replace the old lighting with LED downlights. It really modernised the home. The electrician also replaced the dated power points with new ones that included USB charging points. This was a great selling point for the property manager and it improved our rent.

Cosmetic makeovers are an important way to improve the cash flow on a property. Another is to make an addition to the property such as a carport. This is a simple and relatively inexpensive way to add garaging. When you think about it, people will pay more rent to have their car under cover than to leave it to the elements. The payback period for a carport is often as little as 18 to 24 months and yet the carport will stand for many years providing valuable cash flow.

Many houses we acquired in the Hunter Valley had two bedrooms and a sleepout. The sleepout was often an enclosed veranda. If a sleepout can be converted into a third bedroom (by adding a wall and a door), it will naturally increase the rent. Investor friends of ours, Ros and Wayne, often bought homes with a large kitchen and separate dining room and then converted the dining room into an extra bedroom as the kitchen had plenty of place for a dining table. People always want more bedrooms and are happy to pay a little more rent for an extra one.

A property we acquired in the Lithgow area had no heating. Lithgow, west of the Blue Mountains in country NSW, is one of those places that experience the extremes of cold in winter and heat in summer. The property manager told us that while you can just about rent a property without a stove in Lithgow you definitely can't if there is no heating. For $2000 we bought and installed a gas heater. The property manager was right: we had people lining up to rent the property. The rent ended up being $40 a week more than first estimated and the payback period on the heater was just 12 months.

Imagine how you can supercharge your rent returns by implementing multiple strategies. It is all about being creative. Always ask yourself how you can improve the performance of the income return on a property. The small things count and whatever you do today will impact positively on your returns for many years to come.

KEY POINTS

1. A cosmetic makeover doesn't have to cost a whole lot to dramatically improve the cash flow on your property.

2. A *payback period* is the length of time required for an investment to recover its initial outlay in terms of profit or savings. For example, if a makeover costs $2500 and you get an increase in rent of $30 per week, the payback period is 18 months.

3. Consider the geographical area of your investment property. Are there specific items that will make your property more rentable, such as heating or cooling in areas with extremes of temperature?

4. You can supercharge your rental returns by implementing multiple strategies.

FELICITY'S INVESTING TIP

Cosmetic makeovers can add thousands to the value of the property and also give you a significant boost in cash flow.

CHAPTER 13

Property Management

The first rule of management is delegation. Don't try and do everything yourself because you can't.
Anthea Turner

Professional vs DIY Landlord

I have done both, however I am huge fan of hiring a professional property manager because a good one will not only save you money but make you money. Their costs range from 4% - 9% of the monthly rent collected, and they are responsible for:

1. **Tenants** - Finding and qualifying a tenant for your property. Most property managers have a current database of qualified tenants that are looking to rent property. In my experience most property managers hate wasting their time having to go to court because a tenant hasn't complied with the rental agreement and therefore are quite motivated to find a good tenant for your property. When they find someone they will often contact the landlord to see if they are happy with the their recommendation. In some cases, where a tenant has not rented before or some part of their application is not strong, they are offered a shorter lease term so that they can be road tested.

2. **Condition Reports** - Preparing a detailed property condition report prior to a tenant taking possession. The tenant has to also sign off on the condition report. If there is damage done to the property, this is the document that will be used to prove that the property is in poorer condition than when handed over to the tenant.

3. Rental Payments - Ensuring rental payments are collected on time and paid to you each month. This task can be time consuming and painful if the tenant stops paying, and it requires someone to be diligent and on top of the payments. The property manager needs to have good communication skills and not fall into the trap of being too nice. There is room for compassion, however there should be very little tolerance for late or missed payments. A tenant that has an inconsistent payment history will more than likely be asked to leave at the end of a lease or evicted for non-payment. It will become increasingly harder for them to secure decent rental accommodation with a poor payment history.

4. Repairs - Managing the wear-and-tear repairs.

5. Smoke Alarms - Ensuring that hard-wired smoke alarms (now compulsory in every rental property) are tested and cleaned every 12 months.

6. Renovations - Recommending tradespeople for repairs and renovations and organising quotes for you if necessary.

7. Insurance Claims - Assisting with insurance claims.

8. Rent Reviews - Recommending rent reviews to keep pace with the market. Many landlords don't increase rent for fear of losing a tenant. The problem is that if they wait several years to increase the rent to market rent, they then lose the tenant because the delayed increase is so big. Small incremental increases to keep pace with the market are highly recommended. The tenant is unlikely to get upset and move because of a small increase. If you think about it, a $10 weekly increase is just $520 a year and most people wouldn't move because moving costs would outweigh the rent increase and it is highly likely that their next property would be at market rent anyway. Tenants are more likely to move because their circumstances change and not because of a rent review to keep pace with the market. Like most people, tenants like stability. They often have kids and it is important that they are close to the networks that support them.

9. **Legal Notices** - Issuing the correct legal notices in the event of non-compliance with any of the conditions in the rental agreement.

10. **Representation in Court** - Representing you in court if the tenant needs to be evicted for non-payment of rent or causing damage. Going to the tribunal courts to get matters sorted can take an extraordinary amount of time. If you are inexperienced and you don't know the system, it can cost you even more time and money if you are unprepared.

Tenants & Occupants: The Good, the Bad and the Ugly

In my experience, most people are good and require very little 'management'. I have managed all of my vendor finance deals and outsourced most of the rental property to a professional. Most people make their payments on time, keep the property in good condition and overall are easy to work with.

On the flip side, literally a handful of people haven't complied and have consumed a great deal of time – usually to manage them out of the property. Bad tenants have certainly tested my ability to manage them. I have heard the same excuses from the same bad occupants countless times!

Sometimes you have to deal with events that are truly left field, not only to do with tenants or occupants, but even involving managing the expectations of the neighbours.

Case Study - Who Stole my Land?

The neighbour at the back of one of my properties asked if they could erect a fence between the two properties. He owned a battle-axe block that he accessed via a driveway that ran along the side of my property. Putting up a dividing fence is ordinarily not a big deal and the cost is usually shared by the two neighbours.

The neighbour said he would take care of the quotes and the erection of the fence. He was in a hurry as he didn't like my tenant, had a falling out with them and, in fact, had been to great lengths to influence the property manager to move them on. The property manager basically told him that the tenants had a right to live there and that it was not for him to say otherwise.

> The fence was erected, but it ended up three quarters of a metre onto my land. The neighbour argued that the fence was erected in the easement which is where the services for his property were and that this made it ok. Talk about men behaving badly!
>
> The simple fact was that the fence was on my land and regardless of the easement and tight access to his property, I was still entitled to have the fence on the boundary. I ordered a survey, something that should have been done in the first place, but we still ended up in court arguing over where the fence should be. Finally, he had to concede and move the fence at his cost to the boundary.

I learnt three important lessons from this experience. First, always get a survey done *prior* to erecting a fence or doing anything that may impact the boundary. An earlier survey would have saved me a lot of grief in this case.

Second, if I hadn't complained about the fence being on my land, I may have eventually lost it under the laws of adverse possession. Adverse possession is a legal principle that enables the occupier of a piece of land to obtain ownership if uninterrupted and exclusive possession of the land for at least 15 years can be proven.

And third, just because someone tells you how they think it should be and why you should compromise, you don't have to accept their premise.

KEY POINTS

1. Always qualify the person you are about to put into your house. Breaking this rule can cost you a lot of time and money getting them evicted from the property.

2. If you need to prove that a tenant has caused damage, a condition report will be used to prove that the property is in a lesser condition than when handed over to the tenant.

3. Set a high standard with regards to rent being paid on time. This is the roof over people's heads and should be the first bill that gets paid. I simply explain to the potential occupant of the house - No Pay No Stay.

4. It is compulsory for your investment property to have hard-wired smoke alarms that are tested and cleaned every 12 months.

5. Always carry out rent reviews. Small incremental increases that keep pace with the market are highly recommended and are unlikely to cause your tenant to move on.

6. Just because someone tells you how they think it should be and why you should compromise, you don't have to accept their premise.

FELICITY'S INVESTING TIP

A good property manager will not only save you money but will make you money. As a property investor, learn to leverage your time as well as your money.

SECTION 4 :
ACCUMULATION

Chapter 14

Build a Great Team

Alone we can do so little; together we can do so much.
Helen Keller

Building a great team around you whilst you are growing a property portfolio is priceless. Trying to know everything about the legal, accounting or any of the many other professions that support you in your quest will drive you to distraction. Always hire people who are smarter than you and expert in their field. It is by far the most efficient way to grow. I have many talented people on my team to whom I owe a huge debt of gratitude for the amazing work they do for me.

Legal

The legal paperwork in any property transaction is vital. Having a good relationship with a solicitor who understands what you are trying to achieve will make your deals successful.

At the time of my very first vendor finance deal, I couldn't find a solicitor that actually knew how to put a contract together. I had the deal, I had purchased the property and I wanted to on-sell it to my colleague who couldn't get bank finance. We had both worked out and agreed on the terms because we both understood how bank loans worked, but trying to get a solicitor to see what we wanted was a whole other story. I spoke to a number of solicitors, most of whom said it couldn't be done because it hadn't been done before. I finally came across a local solicitor who came up with the idea of a delayed settlement where my colleague could move in straightaway and pay what we had discussed, then refinance once he had built up enough deposit. It wasn't exactly what we wanted but it allowed us to get the deal done.

I eventually came across a lawyer in Sydney who understood that we needed a contract that would allow us to sell a property to people who wanted to pay by instalment and not by traditional lump sum. Tony (Anthony) Cordato did some research and found out that a very common way to sell real estate in Australia prior to the 1960's used a 'terms (instalment) contract'. A lot of the land in Australian cities was sold by developers using a terms contract because back then banks didn't lend to people to buy land. My grandfather acquired land in Sydney's Lane Cove on a terms contract and eventually was able to raise a bank loan to build his own home.

I soon discovered how important it was to have a lawyer that could draw up other documents as well. As my vendor finance business grew, I needed to work with joint venture partners in order to acquire more stock. Eventually you run out of the ability to finance large numbers of properties and you need to work with other people to continue to raise finance. I once again called on Tony to draw up a joint venture agreement. Basically, the deal was that I did all the work putting the deal together and managing it and an investor partner put down the deposit and qualified for the loan to purchase the property. We shared the profits and any losses if they arose - fortunately they were minimal.

Accounting

I also needed a proactive accountant, not just someone that would pull the financials together at the end of the financial year and submit them to the tax office. I needed someone that understood property investment and could advise me on what structures I needed to protect my assets and discuss with me the best way to grow. I remember being really nervous because I felt like I was just a small fish when I called Bruce Whiting from Business Artisans to see if he would be my accountant. I wasn't a big time investor, I was just someone that had a huge desire to be a property investor. Bruce was impressive from the first moment I spoke to him. He had a comprehensive understanding in all areas of property investing, advanced structures and tax planning. He made some enquires about my current position and suggested setting up a company trust structure for the next few deals. As I grew, Bruce was there to help with advice and practical strategies and he is still my trusted advisor in all things accounting.

Bookkeeping

One of my first employees was a bookkeeper and an extremely important member of the team. I was very fortunate to find Kylie Richards from Balance the Books. Kylie set up MYOB and wrote systems for setting up clients, collection of payments and statements along with the general running of the day-to-day business. Whilst I have had bookkeepers come and go, the manuals that Kylie set up have withstood the test of time.

Conveyancer

I have also found it advantageous to have a conveyancer as well as a lawyer on my team, especially for property acquisitions. You can do 'DIY' conveyancing and, yes, you can save on the cost, but at the end of the day, you can't be an expert in that field as well.

Mortgage Broker or Banker

Having a mortgage broker or banker on your team is vital. One of the reasons for developing my mortgage brokering business was to service property investors. Some of the biggest gripes I hear from my property investors is that they feel they are not understood by their bank and just when they finally develop a good relationship, their banker is transferred or leaves the position. Property investors building a portfolio have a different set of needs and wants compared to, say, a first home buyer or someone looking for a good refinance deal. The following are the top five mistakes property investors make when it comes to finance:

1. **Not getting the right advice** or worse still taking advice from people with zero experience. How often have you heard a story like the one about the uncle (three times removed!) who had once owned an investment property ….? The rest of the story is usually that everything that could gone wrong did go wrong: the tenants stopped paying and just before abandoning the property they trashed it and

then as soon as it was repaired it burnt to the ground. Yes, things do go wrong, however if you seek good advice and education on property investment it is soon apparent that you can mitigate many of the associated risks. For example, you can get landlord insurance that can cover rent default and malicious damage and building insurance in case of fire. It is not all doom and gloom. Property investment is a skill and takes the correct advice and education to hone it.

2. **Shopping around for finance** – it sounds like a good idea but what is really happening is that your credit report is now starting accumulate 'footprints' from all the lenders that you have approached. This then impacts the decision of the lender that you finally decide to work with. Many loans get refused purely on the basis of too many credit enquiries. Employ an experienced mortgage broker to make enquiries for you that will not impact on your credit report. A mortgage broker has the ability to go behind the scenes and make all the enquires you need without the enquiry being recorded on your credit report. Obtaining credit has become quite complex, so leave it to the professionals do a good job for you.

3. **Not correctly structuring finance** – Many lenders will 'cross collateralise' properties. This means that the collateral from one property is used as collateral to acquire a loan for another property. The impact of having the properties crossed is that the acquisition of more properties becomes quite difficult. You are also at the mercy of the lender that has all your business. If you want to use the equity of your current property to buy an investment property, the best structure is to open up a line of credit for the equity that you wish to tap into. For example, say you own a property worth $500,000, currently owe $300,000 on your home loan and want $100,000 released so that you can put deposits down and pay closing cost for a new purchase. One of the best structures is to have the loan 'split' where $300,000 remains, usually as a principal and interest reducing loan, and the

split loan is a line of credit loan. That way you have separated the non-deductible debt (debt that cannot claimed as an expense on your tax return) from deductible debt (debt that may be claimed as an expense on your tax return). If you simply 'top up' the $300,000 home loan to $400,000, there is no clear line between your non-deductible debt and your deductible debt.

4. **Too much debt and not enough debt reduction** – All too often people get excited and want to gear or leverage their properties to dangerously high levels without any thought as to how they are going to reduce the debt. The thinking here is that they are hoping the properties will increase in value and eventually pay out the debt, but what if the properties don't go up in value? Interest only loans may be a useful tool for growing a property portfolio, but there still needs to be some debt reduction component to the overall portfolio. The first debt that needs to be reduced is the non-deductible debt, better known as consumer debt, usually a home or car loan and credit cards. Refinancing and wrapping up your car loans and credit cards into the home loan sounds like a good idea as most people like that the monthly repayment will be reduced. But think about this: if you wrap up your maxed-out credit card with last night's dinner bought with it, you will be paying last night's dinner back over 30 years! A properly structured debt elimination plan is always a much better choice than simply wrapping up debt every few years. You will never own your home doing that. It also indicates that you are living beyond your means and need to address your spending, not cover up the bad habit with constantly rolling it up into your home loan.

5. **Using your current bank for all your needs** – You may have been a client of a bank since you were five years old when your parents first set you up with a little bank account to get you in the savings habit. Eventually you grow up and you want to buy your first home so you naturally go to the bank that has your saving account to approach them for a

loan. The big mistake here is that no two banks are the same although from the outside looking in they may appear to be. If you are an aspiring property investor you want lenders that can meet specific criteria on your proposed purchase. You don't want to be locked in to one bank's policy; you want flexibility to use different lenders so that you can take advantage of good lending deals.

Insurance Broker

I first hired an insurance broker simply because I needed specific insurance for vendor finance contracts as landlord's insurance didn't meet our needs. The insurance broker was instrumental in getting an underwriter to prepare a specialised policy for vendor finance. It was very convenient to have a broker look after all our insurance needs. At first, I used to groan at the broker fee on each policy, but that was before something went wrong. We had a claim and the insurance company said No. This was when I saw how valuable it was to have an insurance broker on our team. We had a property that was badly trashed to the tune of $30,000 and it was a huge shock to be told that the insurance company wasn't going to pay out. The broker stepped in and spent months in negotiation with the insurance company until the issue was resolved. I have never whinged or groaned about the broker fee again. In fact, I just smile now - they are worth their weight in gold.

Real Estate Agent

An engaged and proactive real estate agent or agents are mandatory on your team. If you have relationships of mutual respect with them, they bring you good deals.

Property Manager

A professional property manager on your team often can make the difference between a property that performs and one that doesn't. See Chapter 13 – Property Management.

Financial Planner

A financial planner will look at various different insurance options to protect your income and your assets. I believe having a financial planner on your team can also be very advantageous when your portfolio has some maturity. Let's face it, the whole goal of going into property investment is to be financially free. This begs the question - once you have a large portfolio, how do you maximise its performance, retire early and make the most of your financial freedom?

Business Mentors

Probably the most important members of my team are my mentors. I wouldn't be where I am today without them. They say that when the student is ready the teacher appears and I can tell you that has been true for me. When I needed property investment knowledge, the opportunity arose. If you want results you need a coach or mentor, like exceptional sports people. Mentoring may be expensive, however it sure beats the cost of ignorance and in most cases what is paid out in mentoring fees comes back in increased revenue many times over.

KEY POINTS

1. Surround yourself with a strong team of professionals; it is vital for the growth of your property portfolio.

2. When the student is ready the teacher appears.

3. Top five mistakes people make when borrowing money

   - Not getting the right advice
   - Shopping around for finance
   - Not correctly structuring finance
   - Too much debt and not enough debt reduction
   - Using your current bank for all your needs

FELICITY'S INVESTING TIP

Always hire people who are smarter than you and expert in their field. Expect to pay them for their advice.

CHAPTER 15

How to Minimise Lag Time

Don't judge each day by the harvest you reap but by the seeds that you plant.
Robert Louis Stevenson

Property investment requires patience as it is for the long term. Lag time is the 'waiting period' between the time you completed a property transaction and the time it starts to yield a return. I love properties that can make monthly cash flow. In other words, all the property expenses including mortgage, rates and insurance are covered by income from the property and there is still money left over.

If you are buying properties for cash flow, you may start out with one property that makes you a very modest income. Because it is not relying on you to contribute to maintain it, you will more than likely acquire a second property in close succession. If this property also makes a modest income, then you will be looking for a third. Of course, this will depend on how much deposit and ability to borrow you have. At first, the income on your first property won't be all that impressive, but as you acquire more properties your income will start to look reasonable. Over time, the rents will increase and so will the value of each property. If you are in the game for a decade or more, you will notice how much each mortgage has reduced and how much the value of each property has increased. You will start to wonder why you hadn't bought more. It just takes time.

Reap What You Sow

This biblical quote is quite apt when you are building a property portfolio. Taking action to get started is the most important thing that you can do today. Many people think that there has to be a 'right time' to get into the market. The right time to get into the market is when the numbers on the property that you want to acquire meet with your expectation. The quicker you can start to acquire property the faster you can 'reap' the rewards down the track. Working on your own personal finances (see SECTION 1 - FOUNDATION) is something you can do today. It can make a dramatic difference so that instead of just getting by, pay cheque to pay cheque, you actually set aside some of your money to build deposits with the view to building a property portfolio so that you can experience financial freedom.

It works both ways, of course. If you don't reap, you won't sow. If you don't take action, your results are going to be non-existent. If you buy property without knowing why and if you don't do any market research, it is quite possible that you will reap nothing but grief. The same goes for your personal finances. If you don't pay attention and instead reject the idea of doing any work on your finances, guess what happens? You end up in a bad financial position. Have you ever heard people say they went bankrupt overnight? In most cases it doesn't happen overnight but starts with a late payment here and another there, the gradual snowballing of bills, no action taken to correct course and 'suddenly' bankruptcy.

Lack of Performance

You may already have a property portfolio that isn't performing the way you thought it would. As Kenny Rogers sang, "You have to know when to hold 'em and know when to fold 'em". I have seen many investors buy a property that doesn't perform. Often the purchase was ill-informed and they bought because it seemed like a good idea at the time, without much knowledge on property investing. When a property isn't performing, the real problem is knowing whether to ride out the situation hoping it will get better. If a property is bleeding you to death and you are struggling to meet the repayments each month, the best thing you can do is sell it. You may have to sell at a loss but at least this will stop the bleeding and sleepless nights. After all, it could take several years for a property to start performing, if it ever does. The quicker you make the decision to sell, the quicker you can move forward to something positive with your property portfolio.

Case Study - Performance

One of my investor clients had a house that just did not perform. He desperately wanted to sell because of a bad experience with the tenant. However, because the house was in a state of disrepair it was difficult for potential buyers to raise finance. He procrastinated for two years, not wanting to spend any money on the house and lowering the sale price repeatedly, to no avail. Every month he forked out for the loan repayment, rates and insurance. The feedback from the agent was that the property needed repairs in order to sell. The only person that could have bought would have been someone that didn't require finance, which limits a seller's market quite substantially.

Eventually, the conclusion was reached to put some much-needed work into the property to make it saleable. Having the property on the market for all that time also damaged the ability to get a decent sale price. The good news is that once it was repaired and had a mini-makeover, it rented like crazy with the rent considerably more than the outgoings. The property will be able to be sold down the track; it just needs to recover from its bad reputation in the market.

The message here is that even though selling would have been the right strategy because the property wasn't performing, the property also needed essential repairs so that the incoming buyer could raise finance on it. If one of your properties isn't selling, ask the agent for feedback. In this case, the feedback was ignored. This cost the investor two years' worth of loan repayments as well as the chance to sell the property immediately, once it was repaired.

Systems

In order to be efficient, I have systems in place to streamline my activities. To implement systems, I worked out and wrote down all the different processes involved in everything from acquiring property to finding and qualifying occupants, from managing payments to finding investors to help fund the purchase of new property. It is surprising just how many processes there are. My main priority is to make sure that I have good bookkeeping systems in place. As mentioned in Chapter 14, Build a Great Team, I was able to hire an excellent bookkeeper who wrote systems on how to set up a new client, how to record the collection of money and how to prepare statements for the occupants and investors.

Knowing what I want to acquire and what numbers I am prepared to pay for property are systems that serve me well. Like a cookie cutter machine, a system makes things very predictable. Knowing my target market allows me to advertise for the people that I want in the homes. When it comes to qualifying people, I have an application form to collect data and systems in place to weed out undesirable prospects.

When I first started out I didn't have any systems, I had just heard about the idea and had a huge desire to get started. I found that whenever I was faced with a problem it usually meant that I needed to implement a system in order to solve it. Once I figured out what needed to be achieved, I set about creating a system so that I wouldn't have to reinvent the wheel.

Joint Venture Partners

There comes a time when you eventually run out of deposit and the ability to service loans. To help shorten the lag time on property transactions, working with joint venture partners can provide a constant flow of deposits and bank finance. I have found this to be the most efficient way to grow a portfolio. It just comes down to my ability to find houses and occupants and to structure deals that make sense to all parties.

Having a track record is very useful when talking to joint venture investors about how a deal would work. People respond well to having a tangible document (I call this an 'investor's pack') to peruse and look at past deals as well as other projects on the horizon. The investor's pack clearly outlines the vision, the property strategy, the joint venture information and the rights and responsibilities of both parties. It includes all the information relating to a specific property and the potential profit.

For my joint ventures, the joint venture partner provides the deposit and qualifies for the loan while I do all the work to set up the deal and manage the deal for as long as it remains in existence. All profits and losses are split 50/50. When seeking out joint venture partners, I start with my personal networks. Many of my joint venture investors are professional people and just don't have the time to actually go out and find a deal. Many joint venture investors want to work with someone experienced who appreciates how much work is involved in setting up a deal, so sharing the deal arrangements is very appealing for them.

Joint ventures are an extraordinarily great way to grow a portfolio or a business quickly. Marrying up money and expertise means that you have plenty of resources that enable you to grow exponentially. Joining forces with a joint venture partner is an advanced strategy and requires high accountability and a high level of trust. Contrary to what most believe, investing is an emotional thing (as discussed in Chapter 16 - Investment Mindset for Growth). Dealing with people's own hard-earned cash, no matter how hard you try, things can get emotional. This is why it is so important to have an agreement that is very clear and to work with a high level of integrity.

KEY POINTS

1. Lag time is the 'waiting period' between the time you complete a property transaction and the time it starts to yield a return.

2. The right time to get into the market is when the numbers on the property that you want to acquire meet with your expectation.

3. "Know when to hold 'em and know when to fold 'em". If a property is bleeding you to death and you are struggling to meet the repayments each month, the best thing you can do is sell it.

4. Creating good systems allows you to replicate with ease, and grow.

5. Good systems are like a cookie cutter machine; the results are very predictable.

6. To help shorten the lag time on property transactions, working with joint venture partners provides the constant flow of deposits and bank finance.

7. Marrying up money and expertise means that you have plenty of resources to grow exponentially.

8. Joining forces with a joint venture partner is an advanced strategy and requires high accountability and a high level of trust.

FELICITY'S INVESTING TIP

Take action today. If you don't make a start, you will never reap rewards. Your first action can be as simple as getting your finances in order or organising finance for a potential purchase.

CHAPTER 16

Investment Mindset for Growth

Our deepest fear is not that we are inadequate. Our deepest fear is that we are powerful beyond measure. It is our light, not our darkness, that most frightens us. Your playing small does not serve the world. There is nothing enlightened about shrinking so that other people won't feel insecure around you. We are all meant to shine as children do. It's not just in some of us; it is in everyone. And as we let our own lights shine, we unconsciously give other people permission to do the same. As we are liberated from our own fear, our presence automatically liberates others.

Marianne Williamson

Having the correct mindset is huge when it comes to property investing. There are so many things that you don't even know about yourself that you learn along the way. I have worked with many aspiring property investors who are keen to get the data and ignore mindset because they simply believe that it doesn't apply to them, often dismissing it as 'woo woo' stuff. Their belief system is that all they need is the data. The problem is that we are human beings with emotions, so when it comes to making good decisions, we have to deal with the emotional part of ourselves. Have you ever noticed that when you are highly stressed and under pressure, no matter how hard you try to work out what to do you can't and the thoughts in your head are like spaghetti? And then when you are completely relaxed and removed from the situation the solution just comes to you?

Tips & Strategies

If you think all you need to aspire to property investment are tips and strategies, you are horribly misled. Tips and strategies only make up 5% of what it takes to be a property investor. They are helpful if you have your niche in place and systems to streamline the acquisition of your properties. I often leave a seminar or workshop with a wonderful nugget of an idea that helps me continually improve what I do. Tips and strategies are designed to do exactly that: improve what you are *currently doing*. I see people try to implement a tip or a strategy without any research and then wonder why it fails. Property investing takes work, a lot of work, but it is rewarding and highly profitable because it is also enjoyable. It is also a business and requires the investor to have strong financial proficiency, sound skills in market research, excellent management skills and control of one's emotions so that good solid business decisions can be made.

Money Management Skills

If tips and strategies make up 5%, money management skills make up the next 15% and are paramount to your success. This is why the first section of this book focuses on money management and getting that foundation correct. If you think about it, anything that is solid has a firm foundation, and property investment is no different. When you have a reliable system in place to keep your personal finances under control so that all your bills are paid on time without fail, you have a lifestyle that doesn't require funding by debt where all the basic stuff is on autopilot so that your mind can be free of that clutter. When your mind is free of clutter and you are organised and in control of your own destiny, you have the ability to be more creative and to identify the opportunities that will present themselves.

Case Study – Opportunity

A wonderful opportunity presented itself to me one day. The agent that I was in constant communication with let me know that she had two houses and a block of land that had been recently subdivided where the vendor wanted to sell the whole lot as one package. The agent was having trouble selling two houses and land as one package as not a lot of people wanted that configuration. The agent knew that I would be interested in the houses and she also knew that I didn't normally buy land. She asked me if I would be interested in making an offer.

I placed an offer to acquire the whole lot at a substantial discount. I knew that I could put the houses into my vendor finance program and on-sell the land quickly at a substantial discount, leave something in for the next buyer and still make money for myself. The vendor accepted my offer and as soon as we exchanged the contracts unconditionally, I asked the agent to sell the land. It was sold the following week. I only held the land in my name for a few weeks and made a profit of $30,000 for my troubles.

The point is that I was in a really good position when that deal came along. I knew my property niche; I had developed good relationships with real estate agents; my personal and business foundations were in place; and I had the finance organised and ready. I did feel lucky, but really there wasn't too much luck at play. I would have never have been in a position to take up the opportunity if I hadn't had everything in place.

Psychology

If tips and strategies make up 5% and money management skills 15% it is psychology and emotion that make up the remaining 80% of what is required to be a property investor. I am reminded daily that there needs to be a *non-emotional* solution for every challenge that presents itself. The reason that many good deals appear on the market is because people's emotions are driving their decisions, such as in many cases of divorce. Many people end up in bad deals for exactly the same reason, namely they are in love with the house, not the numbers.

I often hear investors complaining about the tax they have to pay once their property is making money. The emotional fear of paying tax is often strong enough to motivate them to sell. But why do we fear paying tax? Only a portion of the money a property makes will go to the tax department and you actually get to keep the rest. It seems crazy to operate out of the misunderstanding that paying tax must be avoided at all costs.

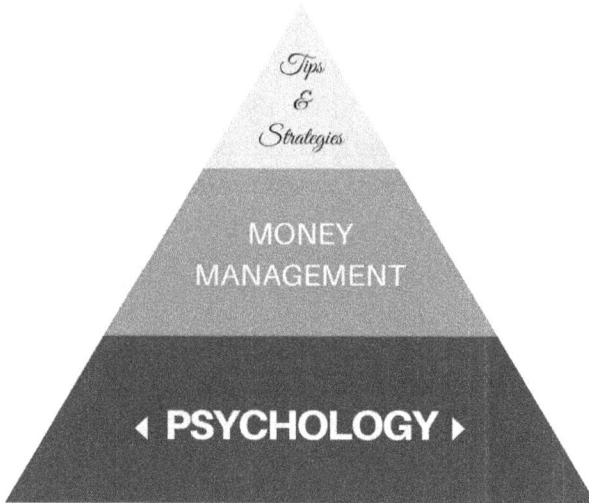

The Human Factor

We can't escape the fact that there are human beings involved in property transactions. Sadly, there are many unethical events that happen in property investment. It is one thing to take the emotion out of a negotiation but it is whole other thing to take advantage of someone that is vulnerable.

I have seen many unethical vendor finance deals. I have seen people take a concept from a weekend seminar and decide to acquire a house for the purpose of putting someone in under a vendor finance contract. With very little research, vulnerable people are signed up with very little qualifying. Such tenants are often relying on social security or in low paid jobs with not a hope of meeting the repayments. They pay deposits because they want the dream of home ownership. Typically, they are soon evicted and lose all their money. In fact, some unscrupulous people make a business out of 'churning' properties and just collecting deposits with little regard for the human beings at the other end of the transaction. This type of behaviour is about getting rich quick. The sad fact is that if an ethical business model was adopted, these so-called investors would make more money than they could have ever imagined, with large numbers of happy clients that constantly refer.

Ethical property investors have a motto that is at the core of their being: CLIENT FIRST ALWAYS. If the client is the focus of the transaction and you exercise due diligence, you will have very few management problems and this in itself is a huge money saver. The most successful property investors are those who do the market research and qualify the occupants, regardless of whether the occupant is a tenant or a potential buyer. They also have strong management procedures in place and procedures for if something goes wrong.

Change is the Only Constant

As mentioned, I started my property investment career in 1999. Many people are curious about why I chose mortgage broking over what most describe as the dream occupation of property investing. Truth be known, I became burnt out and exhausted because I didn't put in enough systems as the business grew. This has probably been my biggest lesson.

In the middle of 2008 I took a two-week break that became an unscheduled two-year sabbatical. I was in the very fortunate position of being able to take the time I needed and I hired a really good bookkeeper to keep things going. I spent a lot of time reading and also had the wonderful opportunity to go to Uganda and Tanzania in East Africa. I specifically wanted to look at how micro-finance programs were helping women in abject poverty build small businesses that not only transformed the lives of their families but also their villages. The thing that struck me most about all these women was how incredibly hopeful about their future, and how proud of the difference they were making. When I came home from that trip in March 2010 I realised that I had rested on my laurels enough and it was time to get into action again … there was still much more to do in my business.

I soon realised that property investors needed an advocate in the finance space. I discovered that many of my investor clients felt that their bank or mortgage broker didn't understand their needs for growing a property portfolio. How could they, after all, if they weren't property investors themselves? On the other hand, I had a strong background in lending and a full understanding of the needs of property investors, so this is what I turned my hand to. With the goal of financial freedom and having chosen investment property as the vehicle, property investors wanted someone that could help them work through their goals and provide the clarity and confidence to keep them on track and growing.

It was shortly after this time, in July 2010, that the National Consumer Credit Protection Act was introduced, requiring people dealing in credit to have a licence. This impacted on how banks lent to people and made it even more complex for people to borrow money. This was an opportunity for me to specialise in helping investors obtain traditional bank finance.

I learnt a couple of very valuable lessons in my time as a vendor financier. The first was to always review my systems and to implement new systems to handle growth. The second was not to spend too long in my comfort zone. I realised that the periods that were the most uncomfortable were the periods when I learnt the most and when the business grew the most. Getting used to constant change is going with the flow. It is a whole lot easier to go with the flow than to put up resistance, which is like trying to swim upstream.

Myth Busting

One of the myths about property investment is that there are certain lucky and successful investors with the Midas touch who never have a problem. In fact, nothing could be further from the truth. The fact is that when you do volume of anything, the risk of something going wrong increases dramatically. What is important is not whether or not you have problems, but how you manage them.

Sometimes the first instinct is to blame, or justify a bad result, or take no responsibility, but none of these are the attitude of a successful investor. A successful investor will always take a proactive approach and will learn from each experience and keep improving systems in order to reduce the number of bad events in the future.

If you are renting or vendor-financing property, the best thing that you can do is make sure you qualify the right people. If you accept someone that is below standard, you increase the risk of not receiving payment and worse still getting the property trashed. Even with the best qualifying, however, occasionally your occupant is hit by a life event, sickness, divorce or job loss, to name a few. It is important to have an attitude of 'soft' towards the person and 'hard' towards the situation. You can still have compassion for someone in hard times but accepting non-payment without a clear plan for getting back on track is never a solution, as it serves neither of you well. Instead, make inquiries into their financial situation and find out how they intend to live for the period of time that they may want you to help them with. It is not acceptable for them to just stop paying. It is one thing to miss a payment and make an arrangement to catch it up, but to miss a series of payments without communicating the reason is a whole different ball game.

Case Study – Head in the Sand

One vendor finance client would regularly stop paying without communicating why, then make a payment arrangement, only to fail to maintain it. She was clearly in hardship but she had her head in the sand, hoping the situation would resolve itself. It turned out that her husband had left her and she was not coping emotionally. After legal notices were served and much angst experienced, we finally came to the decision that the property would be sold to repay the debt and she could move on with the surplus funds from the sale. The agent that sold the house organised a property for the client to rent in the same suburb so that her kids could stay at the same school and she could remain close to her parents, as this was her priority. She was relieved in the end, but it was difficult for her to face reality because she was in high stress.

What is important is the way that we view a situation and then make the decision to manage a problem. I am reminded of what Dev Patel (the hotel manger in the movie *The Best Exotic Marigold Hotel*) said: "Everything will be all right in the end. If it's not all right, then it's not the end."

Case Study – Fraud

I was the victim of fraud in December 2012. I wanted to grow the mortgage business and thought it would be a good idea if I bought another broker's 'trail book' (mortgage brokers receive a trailing commission for each loan they write, recorded in what is known as a trail book). I received regular emails from a company advertising that they were trail book brokers. Everything appeared legitimate right down to the trust account to pay the deposit into. When I eventually figured out that I had been hoodwinked, my first reactions were anger, embarrassment and feeling helpless. I lost a sizeable amount of money and whilst the loss was not catastrophic, it hurt. After I finally came to the conclusion that I wasn't going to get my money back, I made the decision to get my money's worth and stop the guy from ripping people off.

I started to make some enquiries to see how many other mortgage brokers had also lost money. To my horror, I found out the guy running the trail book brokerage company had been operating for a number of years and that very little had been done to stop him. I found a couple of industry press articles warning brokers about the scam, but nobody had actually taken a stand to stop him.

After seeking legal advice, I was encouraged to lodge a fraud report with the local police, however for anyone to take me seriously I needed other brokers who were victims to also lodge fraud reports. I set about finding other brokers, and as it turned out this wasn't too difficult because this guy had ripped off a lot of people. I connected with a broker in Melbourne who had also lost money and he was on a similar path to me, locating other brokers and convincing them to lodge fraud reports. Together we located 15 other brokers who each lodged fraud reports. Finally, we got a phone call from the Victorian Fraud Squad saying that they would now investigate the allegations. The guy was arrested then let out on bail. He reoffended and is now back in jail. He was eventually found guilty, whilst his jail term is relatively short his prospects to live in the outside world are dim at best.

The one thing that I am proud of is taking a stand. I know that if we as a group hadn't stood up to this guy, he would have continued his modus operandi and ripped off more people. I actually felt much better about the situation once I had mentally let go of the money and taken the appropriate action of lodging a fraud report.

I share this story to encourage those who may be caught up in a similar situation. Being ripped off does not mean you are stupid or in the wrong. It just means you trusted someone and they took advantage of you. With the right mindset, you can put it behind you and move ahead.

KEY POINTS

1. When investing in property, having the right mindset will help you through the good times and the bad.

2. Never make big decisions when your emotions are high because you won't be thinking clearly. High emotion equates to low intelligence. Make important decisions when calm.

3. Many people believe that tips and strategies are all you need to be a good property investor. Tips and strategies only make up 5% of the equation. Money management is very important but only makes up the next 15%. Psychology and emotions make up the remaining 80%.

4. Operate with ethics and integrity. The ethical property investors have a motto that is at the core of their being – CLIENT FIRST ALWAYS.

5. You don't get to rest on your laurels just because you did some good work. There are always new challenges and new problems to solve.

6. Along with death and taxes, change is the only constant. Get used to being out of your comfort zone in order to grow.

7. A successful property investor *never*:

    • lays blame

    • justifies a bad result

    • fails to take responsibility

8. If things go wrong, particularly with a non-paying tenant, being soft on the person hard on the situation is likely to get the situation resolved quickly.

FELICITY'S INVESTING TIP

Don't stay in your comfort zone for too long – you grow more when you are outside your comfort zone.

CHAPTER 17

Final Words

Thank you for taking the time to read the *Extraordinary Property Investing*. I trust you have found the stories, strategies and tips helpful and inspiring. Financial intelligence and competence elude a good number of people, but you don't have to be one of them. I hope my book has offered you a path towards your own financial freedom. I know that this information has transformed my life and I have since seen it transform the lives of many people around me. The important next step is for you is to **take action now**.

Think about this for a moment. Imagine that the action you took is to set up your finances on auto pilot so that you can predict with absolute certainty and excitement what the extraordinary results will be. Imagine that your next action is to start market research and that you discover that there are great deals in the market place. Imagine the action of approaching your banker or mortgage broker and finding that it *is* possible to start acquiring these great deals. It all comes back to a single decision: you can decide not to do anything or you can decide to take action. If you decide to continue what you are currently doing, then you can guarantee the results are going to be the same. Change what you are doing and you will change destination.

We only get one opportunity at life, so it is worth playing full out and seeing what is possible even if it seems completely impossible at first glance. The key to growing a property portfolio for financial freedom is to start with baby steps and keep at it. If you make a mistake, don't waste the lesson by beating yourself up, but ask yourself what you have learned.

When you feel uncomfortable doing something for the first time, stick with it. The discomfort is a sign that you are in a growth phase and as a result of the growth phase you should see results. It is always nice to take a breather and relax, and I highly recommend taking time out to smell the roses. Personally, I can attest to the importance of then getting back into the action and taking on challenges to inspire and excite you again. Sometimes when frustration sets in, it just means you are very close to a break through, so don't give up.

It is time now to take action and get started on *your* journey towards financial freedom.

NEXT STEPS

If you have enjoyed the book and want to learn more, go to felicityheffernan.com.au. Here you will find information on up-coming property investment events. These events are packed with powerful information to help you on your property investment journey. Felicity also runs regular rendezvous meetings for property investors to network. Details are on the website.

If you would like a free consultation on how to borrow money to grow a property portfolio or how to save thousands on your home loan, please contact Felicity's office by phoning 1800 146 637 or via the web site propertyloanadvisor.com.au. There also free calculators, everything from how much you can borrow to budget planning and informative Blog posts.

Felicity would love to know how you are going, so please share your stories on facebook.com/PropertyLoanAdvisor/ you never know who you will inspire…

About Felicity heffernan

Felicity Heffernan is the founder and CEO of Property Loan Advisor. She helps clients obtain finance to grow a successful property portfolio.

Felicity is a remarkable woman who has achieved what most people would consider impossible. Starting out with a practical plan of action and a burning desire to learn about property investment, she acquired 151 houses in just 10 years. Felicity is also the author of *Extraordinary Property Investing* where she shares her story and the four key principles behind every successful property investor.

Felicity is a woman on a mission with the passion, experience and the desire to share a system to improve the lives of people who want financial independence. Felicity is also a popular keynote speaker for property investor groups in Australia and the USA.

Her presentations are entertaining, engaging and informative and draw on her own property investing journey as she shares powerful lessons learnt along the way.

Felicity is known as a modern-day pioneer in the vendor finance property investment niche. Currently advising on vendor finance and a member of the National Executive Committee for the Finance Brokers Association of Australia, Felicity is a strong advocate for lifting the general level of financial competence among Australians.

www.ingramcontent.com/pod-product-compliance
Lightning Source LLC
Chambersburg PA
CBHW070731220326
41598CB00024BA/3390